The Hero's Fall I Fell For

Jazz Poems

The Hero's Fall I Fell For

Jazz Poems

Dave Oliphant

ALAMO BAY PRESS
SEADRIFT•AUSTIN

Copyright © 2017 by Dave Oliphant

All rights reserved. No part of this book may be reproduced in any form without permission in writing from the publisher, except by a reviewer who may quote brief passages in a review.

Cover illustration:
Book Design: ABP

For orders and information:
Alamo Bay Press
825 W 11th Ste 114
Austin, Texas 78701
mick@alamobaypress.com
www.alamobaypress.com

Library of Congress Control Number: 2017947585
ISBN: 978-1-943306-09-1

In Memory of Harold Meehan
who opened my ears

Contents

- 1   Introduction & Discography

       Part One: Jazz Poems
- 11   from "The Cowtown Circle"
- 13   from "Presidential Doggerel"
- 15   from "Jazz God & Freshman English"
- 17   from "Teachers at South Park High"
- 19   Carroll Black, Author of *Stephen Hero*
- 22   Denton
- 24   Letter to Dave Hickey
- 26   from *Austin*
- 29   Improvisations on the Notes of Akiko Yamaguchi
- 32   from "Music History"
- 35   Five Versions of the "Twelfth-Street Rag"
- 43   Three Hayseed Musicians
- 45   Two Sonnets
- 46   A Wedding Sestina
- 49   Leaders
- 51   The Hero's Fall I Fell For
- 64   Martyrs
- 65   Graduation Day at Stateville Penitentiary
- 68   Ornette in Rome
- 71   from "Nixon"
- 77   Professor Douglass Parker Keeps Charlie Live at the Harry Ransom Center
- 80   Three Musicians Perform Their Freedom
- 83   María's Radio
- 85   On Visiting NYC

90	Jazz by the Boulevard
92	from "Community Music Fest"
94	Boat House Grill
98	Serenading the Neighbors

Part Two: from *KD: a Jazz Biography*

101	Vikings in Reverse
120	O-Yo-De-Lay-Hee-Hoing
128	Westering
136	Arriving
153	Zodiacing
162	Expiring

165	Acknowledgments
167	About Dave Oliphant

The Hero's Fall I Fell For

Introduction & Discography

In 1995, when the University of Texas Press was preparing to publish my historical study, *Texan Jazz*, the senior editor expressed an interest in having a CD sampler of performances by Texas jazz musicians as part of the publication. Because the time required to obtain permissions would delay the scheduled release of the book, it was decided not to wait, and so no CD was included. Ever since then I regretted that such a recording was not available to readers of the book. Twenty years later, in March 2015, after giving a presentation on Texan jazz at Midwestern State University in Wichita Falls, during which I read some of my poems on the music, it occurred to me that I should collect in one volume my short jazz-related poems and certain excerpts from my two book-length poems, *Austin* (1985) and *KD: a Jazz Biography* (2012). As I began to compile the poems, I also thought that I should put together a sampler of performances by some of the jazz figures mentioned in the poetry. The result is this combination of my printed poems and recordings by some of jazz's major exponents, published by Alamo Bay Press during the 100th anniversary of the first recordings of jazz by the Original Dixieland Jazz Band, produced on February 26, 1917, in the studios of the Victor Talking Machine Company in Camden, New Jersey. Although no recording from that first session by the ODJB is included in the accompanying CD, there is a version of the band's 1918 "At the Jazz Band Ball," as later performed in 1927 by cornetist Bix Beiderbecke, which demonstrates the influence of that Nick LaRocca-Larry Shields tune within the development of jazz as an art form.

 The poems in *The Hero's Fall I Fell For* were written and published in magazines and/or books over a span of fifty-two years, from 1964 to 2016. My self-published chapbook of 1962, *doubt & Redoute*, bears the subtitle "A Search for Congeniality," which, as a note at the back of that collection makes clear, is a reference to "Congeniality," a tune by Texas jazzman Ornette Coleman, recorded by his quartet in 1959. The first poem of mine to include a specific reference to a jazz musician (Texas trombonist Jack Teagarden) is

"Letter to Dave Hickey," from 1964, a poem that is not primarily about jazz, as is the case with other selections, but only alludes to the music in the midst of a meditation on issues of the day. A number of the poems in *The Hero's Fall* are about relatives, friends, and high school teachers, and several were written during the late 1960s and very early 1970s, with "Leaders" of 1970 alluding to the Vietnam War and "The Hero's Fall" of 1971 to the Black Power and Back-to-Africa movements of those conflictive years. The excerpts from "Nixon"—my poem on the Texas town of that name; on the U.S. President and his wife Pat; on Dr. Pat Ireland Nixon, a native of Old Nixon, Texas, a physician, and the author of *A History of the Texas Medical Association*; and on Black physician Dr. Lawrence A. Nixon of Marshall, Texas—refer to several jazz musicians and relate thematically to the history of politics and medicine traced in the work's five-line stanzas. In many cases, the poems only mention the names of jazz musicians, but in others they describe the musicians and/or their performances. In the hindsight of putting together this collection, I can see that from early on jazz figured significantly in my writing, no matter what may have been the principal subject of any particular poem. For me, in whatever context it appears, jazz stands for a pearl of great value in contrast to so much in life that seems not worth the price we pay.

    The fact that so many jazz musicians and their music entered my poetry is a testament to the variety and significance of the art form and its artists. This does not mean, however, that my allusions or tributes to the music and its musicians represent "jazz poetry" as such. For this reason I have never felt that it would be appropriate, or effective, to read my poems aloud while jazz was being performed. In most cases the poems of mine that refer to jazz are in forms that do not, it seems to me, lend themselves to a comparison with jazz or to being delivered in conjunction with a performance of the music. Although the poems that mention jazz have themselves taken a variety of forms, none is perhaps "jazzy" in itself. Rather, I have tried through my poetry to pay homage to the art of jazz and to its musicians, whose lives and performances have long been a source of pleasure, inspiration, and solace. A number of the recordings included in the accompanying CD still send shivers up my spine or bring tears to my eyes, above all Duke Ellington's "Merry-Go-Round" and Bunk Johnson's "Weary Blues."

As a Texan, I was aware on beginning to listen to jazz that there were important musicians from various parts of my native state who figured prominently in the history of the music. A number of these musicians appear in my poems, from Jack Teagarden and Jimmy Giuffre to Red Garland, Kenny Dorham, David "Fathead" Newman, and Ornette Coleman, but an equal and larger group hails from other states of the nation; indeed, the greatest names in the history of jazz are among those alluded to, from Bunk Johnson, King Oliver, Louis Armstrong, and Bix Beiderbecke to Duke Ellington, Count Basie, Jimmie Lunceford, Lester Young, Dizzy Gillespie, Charlie Parker, Miles Davis, Charles Mingus, and John Coltrane. Although I could be accused of mere name dropping, I hope that the reference to so many jazz musicians will be taken simply as evidence of my deep appreciation for them and their music.

In collecting the poems, I have ordered them generally in the order in which they were written, although in some cases the poems were written long after the occasions that eventually triggered the writing. The opening excerpts from "The Cowtown Circle" refer to my father's love of jazz, which I only discovered during high school when I brought home recordings that I had purchased as a result of having first heard and tried to perform the music. The second excerpt, from "Jazz God & Freshman English," concerns my high school orchestra and "stage-band" teacher, who introduced me to the music. My 1967 poem written on five jazz performances of a single tune, the "Twelfth Street Rag," prepared me, without at the time my knowing that it did, for writing 29 years later my historical study, *Texan Jazz*, and also for writing 45 years later my book-length poem, *KD: a Jazz Biography*, on the life and music of trumpeter Kenny Dorham. In between "Five Versions of the 'Twelfth Street Rag'" and *KD*, I would write the title poem of the present collection, also on the life of a jazz musician, Joe "King" Oliver, but a much shorter piece than the verse biography of Dorham. The six revised "cantos" out of seventeen from *KD* excerpted here provide a capsule version of Dorham's career, yet hopefully enough about his biography and recordings to allow readers to appreciate why it was that I cast his life and music in verse.

As for the jazz recordings on the enclosed CD, some were produced over 75 years ago, placing them, to my mind, in the public domain. The rest are at least 50 years old, except for Texan Marvin "Hannibal" (Peterson) Lokumbe's "Change Is Coming Soon," from 1993, for which I obtained permission to reproduce the piece from the musician himself. Since there is only one recording by each musician, with the exception of second works by Duke Ellington and Count Basie (three of the four over 75 years old), I felt that such a limited sampling should fall under the practice of "fair use." It is my view that the rights holders should find that in my giving credit to the specific source of each work on the CD that I have aided in advertising their recordings and thereby have encouraged the acquisition by interested readers and listeners of the complete album from which any selection was taken. Also, I believe that it is important that the cultural heritage that jazz represents should be made available in the context of a work like my collection of poetry, without the onerous restrictions wrought by copyright that benefit not the artists or the nation but those who profit from the creative efforts of others. Furthermore, there is no profit from a book of poetry such as mine, and many of the performances on the CD can already be heard on the internet, through YouTube, Spotify, and other on-line downloads. Here, then, are the poems and the corresponding recordings, with track numbers for the compact disc:

from "The Cowtown Circle"

    1. Duke Ellington, "Merry-Go-Round" (Columbia, *I Like*

Jazz), recorded April 30, 1935 (2:59)

2. Jimmie Lunceford, "Lunceford Special" (Kaz Records, *Jimmie Lunceford: The Classic Tracks*), a tune arranged by Texan Eddie Durham, recorded December 14, 1939 (2:51)

3. Benny Goodman, "Jam Session" (Columbia, *I Like Jazz)*, recorded from a 1937 radio broadcast, with Harry James on trumpet (2:41)

from "Jazz God & Freshman English"

4. Dizzy Gillespie, "A Night in Tunisia" (*The RCA Victor Encyclopedia of Recorded Jazz*, Album 5: Gil to Hig), recorded February 22, 1945, with Don Byas on tenor sax (3:08)

"Carroll Black, Author of *Stephen Hero*"

5. Modern Jazz Quartet, "Versailles (Porte de Versailles)" (Atlantic, *Fontessa*), recorded January 22, 1956 (3:27)

"Denton"

6. Euel Box Quintet, "Toddlin'" (Columbia Transcriptions, *North Texas State College Jazz Concert*), recorded 1957 (3:12)

7. Shorty Rogers and His Giants, "Planetarium" (Atlantic, *Martians Come Back!*), recorded March 26, 1955, with Texan Jimmy Giuffre on tenor sax (3:39)

from "Austin"

    8. Ornette Coleman, "Congeniality" (Atlantic, *The Shape of Jazz to Come*), recorded May 22, 1959, with Don Cherry on pocket trumpet (6:48)

"Improvisations on the Notes of Akiko Yamaguchi"

    9. Miles Davis Quintet, "I Could Write a Book" (Columbia, *Relaxin' With Miles*), recorded October 26, 1956, with Texan Red Garland on piano (5:11)

"Five Versions of the 'Twelfth Street Rag'"

    10. Louis Armstrong & His Hot Seven, "Twelfth Street Rag" (Columbia, *Louis Armstrong: The Hot Fives & Hot Sevens,* Vol. 2), recorded May 11, 1927 (3:10)

    11. Duke Ellington, "Twelfth Street Rag" (Decca, *The Original Decca Recordings: Early Ellington*), recorded January 14, 1931 (2:58)

    12. Fats Waller & His Rhythm, "Twelfth Street Rag" (Pickwick International Records, *Ain't Misbehaving*), recorded June 24, 1935 (2:45)

    13. Count Basie, "Twelfth Street Rag" (Jazz Roots, *Jumpin' at the Woodside*), recorded April 5, 1939 (3:08)

"The Hero's Fall I Fell For"

    14. King Oliver, "Too Late" (RCA Victor, *King Oliver in New York*), recorded October 8, 1929 (3:13)

15. Bunk Johnson, "Weary Blues" (Good Time Jazz, *Bunk Johnson and His Superior Jazz Band*), recorded June 11, 1942 (2:46)

"Professor Douglass Parker Keeps Charlie Live at the Harry Ransom Center"

16. Charlie Parker Quintet, "Donna Lee" (Savoy, *The Immortal Charlie Parker*), recorded 1947, with Miles Davis on trumpet (3:02)

from "Music History"

17. Count Basie, "Taps Miller" (Best of Jazz, *Count Basie: His Best Recordings 1936-1944*), recorded December 6, 1944 (3:24)

"María's Radio"

18. Hannibal (Peterson) Lokumbe, "Change Is Going to Come" (Muse Records, *One With the Wind*), recorded September 3, 1993 (4:30)

"Jazz by the Boulevard"

19. David "Fathead" Newman, "Hard Times" (Collectables, *Fathead*), released in 1958, with Ray Charles on piano (4:43)

from "Community Music Fest"

20. Bix Beiderbecke, "At the Jazz Band Ball" (Columbia, *The Bix Beiderbecke Story,* Vol. 1), recorded October 5, 1927 (2:52)

from *KD: a Jazz Biography*

21. Jack Teagarden, "I'm an Old Cowhand" (Mosaic Records, *The Complete Okeh and Brunswick Bix Beiderbecke, Frank Trumbauer, and Jack Teagarden Sessions [1924-36]*), recorded June 15, 1936 (3:08)

22. Kenny Dorham, "I'm an Old Cowhand" (Xanadu Records, *The Kenny Dorham Memorial Album*), recorded January 10, 1960 (4:12)

Part One:
Jazz Poems

from "The Cowtown Circle"

in '41 Kelly Fearing had in explor-
ing an attic found a shadeless lamp
its nude torso missing porcelain el-
bow to armpit the wires once held

he too reproducing an old newspa-
per but his of black white gray on
canvas with headline upside down
Germa[ny] attacks Russians Japan

invades again two ties drape above
from coat hanger instead of a neck
with lives ending or interrupted by
cruel racist world gone power mad

but before the *Attic Piece* had done
in birth year his '39's *Jitterbuggers*
with its girls' swinging skirts show-
ing their knees & a red panty of one

such dances Mom & Dad had saved
up for awaited each week to drive to
or ride with friends & hear big bands
out at Lake Worth his favorite Duke

at times would just stand next to him
& watch as pianist with drums guitar
& bass would hit together on *Merry-
Go-Round* & also *Rockin' in Rhythm*

& partial also to Jimmie's *Lunceford
Special* with its high trumpet work &
stirring trombone of Trummy Young
Joe Thomas with that booming tenor

never said if Harry James a member
of the first band its Casino Ballroom
hired when George Smith the owner
objected to that future trumpet star's

blasting with gusto & had its leader
seat him back behind the other men
but paid him quite a sum in years to
come for that golden horn out front

no need to say they would not have
gone on East Rosedale for listening
to an Ornette Coleman brand of Be-
bop much less his Harmolodic licks

yet neither to express any prejudice
like most from their Depression age
just didn't care for the '40s' sounds
a New Generation had begun to dig

from "Presidential Doggerel"

Harry Truman

on Aunt Sis's carpet
we cousins all played
with pick-up sticks
built houses of cards

& by then could read
the newspaper reports
of the count in Korea
of MIGs shot down

from then remember
first feeling anger
at his having fired
General MacArthur

on his crossing of
the demilitarized zone
only years later would find
Harry had formed a part

of the Kansas City machine
bootlegging in Prohibition
a nightlife attracted & hired
many a Texas jazz musician

"Hot Lips" Budd & Buster
blues men & women too
with their chorded notes
made up for broken laws

in '45 had learned letters
& words on Dick & Jane

not yet of buck-stops-here
or a lonely decision made

to mushroom human skin
but later perhaps to read
when the front page said
he'd not been re-elected

in bold mistaken headline
before the counting done
morning edition declaring
Thomas Dewey had won

once caught from early TV
his daughter Margaret sing
maybe at Constitution Hall
her smiling poppa beaming

light off of glasses gleaming
with he himself at the piano
his tough talk if as blinding
still strong right or wrong

from "Jazz God & Freshman English"

Harold T. Meehan

from the day you came to the high school band hall
needing a 3rd chair trumpet to take Wayne's place
when at the time I was sitting eleventh in line
my hearing ever since hasn't been the same

had prayed for real that every better player
would turn down that lowest of parts
practiced only before or after classes
for the one big blast each spring & fall

not counting the football Friday nights
for autumn sock hops on lips so shot
from marching & blowing half-time shows
till at last you arrived at the awaited name

o perfect you never were
far from it the way you'd breathe
after a soccer game of fifty minutes
winded by all the fags you'd puff

or once on leaving your jumbled home
quietly without a word the record going
you on the couch passed out from mixing
vodka with the bebop licks of Dizzy & Bird

when couples wanted the "stage band" to do
current hits like Elvis's "Hound Dog"
you'd give them "Stars Fell on Alabama"
& plenty of muttered go-to-hells

after rehearsal of dull Irons & Sousa trios
you'd offer the miracle of Beethoven's 1st

the puzzling wartime 5th of Shostakovich
even *Lust for Life* with Quinn & Douglas

that film seen with the orchestra teacher
when you drove to your student's home
a grown man inviting me just imagine
a pimply-faced sophomore seated last chair

to be lowered together down creaking mines
seeing tulip rows sprout from oil paint tubes
squeezed by some guy unheard of till then
some Vincent Van Gogh sliced off his ear

your classics through the bore of a Bach 7 C
as lips touched to life that metal mouthpiece
a Martin horn unlocked by your magic key
would open up a world of unending sound

o invitation to more than music or movie
from sunflowers ragged on canvas stalks
to printed pages with lines by William Blake
his blooms hanging heavy in two quatrains

an imagery would lead to dreams of love
to the writing & revising deep in the night
for appearance in the obscure magazines
closed down as would be South Park High

& the grade
o yes almost forgot
the course went for
no credit

from "Teachers at South Park High"

Harold Meehan

was famous for his mercurial Irish moods
slamming down in disgust a stubby baton
on the stenciled music stand when woods

or strings missed his cue not coming in on
time but then on retuning a violin he'd tell
an anecdote a joke on himself the passion

subdued yet to rise again all knew so well
followed by the deep regret endeared him
at least to those placed him on a pedestal

for sounds he brought to life a Beethoven
1st Gershwin's Parisian horns Diz & Bird
buying the Rugolo *Adventures in Rhythm*

with school-system funds swing unheard
till he'd left his St. Louis home with Bop
in tow scatting notes spreading the word

of syncopation rehearsing for a sock hop
Saturday nite though stock arrangements
like "Jersey Bounce" a far cry from pop-

tune rock by a swiveling pelvis students
adored even with dance a sin in the Bible
belt his job saved by the superintendent's

winking at his drinking doing so a while
yet firing him at last who improvised on
sax blew young minds to jazz & classical

James Manning

had it been an elective unrequired to graduate
whoever would have chosen to take from him
his course with a title warned will regurgitate

dissecting frogs learned as blue jay the mean-
ing of dotted monarch wings biology's bitter
pill even with a microscopic lens for looking

at amoeba could he see a thing would wonder
if through his thickest of glasses he ever saw
the miniscule labels for ear's stirrup hammer

or anvil whose cochlear tubing made to draw
apathetic as to any stapes or canals had rather
hear & play the beguine notes of Artie Shaw

knowing was near or farsighted didn't matter
not at all just wanted eye-finger coordination
to read & perform the parts as a second chair

can't remember if he taught equine evolution
from three-toed into a single hoof or thought
Darwin mistaken & held to a special creation

by then science knew the DNA if he brought
it up tested spelling of enzyme chromosome
don't recall just phoning a neighbor's daugh-

ter for a Saturday date later for senior prom
trying to adapt to make the natural selection
be different with all cells of the same system

Carroll Black: Author of *Stephen Hero*

had come to Lamar Tech from Orange
a city just inside the Texas line
that invisible border through bayous
& beyond it to Cajun wilds

his hometown reached by a highway lifted
up & over the Neches River
tankers below heading out for the Gulf
or inland to port as they floated beneath

that "rainbow" bridge with its black gold view
to scummy weeds   at night the soaring flames
burning off the gas   nothing close to his prose
his retouched portraits of Dedalus or Bloom

for even as a freshman his one ambition
to write another *Ulysses*
how he'd found the classics   reared in swamps
the biggest mystery of that mystical year

mother swore his underwear trimmed with lace
the Ds he made in German bothered much more
couldn't square his Buck Mulligan manner with
the grades he pulled   on clarinet seated last chair

from here he comes in clear   waiting for class
leaning against a hallway wall in his black rayon suit
a silk white shirt   re-reading *Dubliners* or *Leaves of Grass*
nearest thing to Joyce's protagonist the college knew

introduced Faulkner & the latest MJQ
loaned the *Fontessa* album & said to listen to
this Harlequin piece   It's the greatest hit
The Commedia dell' Arte through a jazz quartet

Hear the four Blacks in tails with their delicate touch
reviving the Italian Renaissance in bluesy tones
heard it echoed off walls of neighboring homes
where crews half-slept till the graveyard shift

spinning the record past two a.m.
repeated how dull our schoolmates were
applied to them all that author had meant
so certain had awakened at Finnegan's words

to a tower overlooked the pains of love
a jetty built by the winds of our wittiness
books piled for the crossing to Paris
exile   definition   refinement   horse piss!

since then have been   not there   but abroad
& it just ain't so   homesick   confused
tortured by doubt   the natives intimidating
with their chants of hands-off politics

no sensitive lines came easy or tough
just a picture of that Liberal Arts hall
superimposed while riding crushed in a bus
straining to catch at the quick foreign phrase

wondering where he was   how the novel progressed
would think of Pierre Menard rewriting Cervantes
curious if Carroll had done it to "The Dead"
continued with my own poor imitations of Yeats

haunted still by his talk of those Irish greats
in winter warmed by memories of *A Portrait*'s first page
till remembrance turned cold as baby tuckoo's bed sheet
hopeless as that blind block of North Richmond Street

but revisited & believed in those Beaumont scenes
of his lounging in the hall with its lighting dim
off discolored walls & unbuffed floors
the books in his hands held mostly for looks

yet let in by him as if through a door
to the wonder of this   a place to fit
a form to fill   boiling of crude down to fuel
the cleansing ethyl for an art to steer

gaining for one raised on bayou or marsh
faith in the refinery as an image can mean
though what he opened stayed closed to him
with his dreams of novels unsoiled by the near

now feeling it more deeply than ever   the failure
of this poem he deserves in return
hope at least for a fellow who led the way
the cliché may follow   'tis better to give than etcetera

Denton

    like every other place
    is Janus-faced
    take its dreamed-of campus Kenton blessed
    near where an only brother bled to death
    on his final trip from picking up a remaining group
    of Green Beret reservists the last to parachute

    delivered them safely then flipped his truck
    on a narrow curve   his stomach crushed
    between the driver's seat & the steering wheel
    for years have grieved with that lonely feel
    of his young life slipping away
    three months after graduation two weeks before his wedding day

    talked Aunt Sis into taking a pilgrimage to its hallowed sounds
    in summer heat to its celebrated tree-cooled grounds
    a home to festivals a division of Columbia Records pressed
    its treasured album has stood the test
    though scratchy & so filled with cuts by imitative combos
    a true aficionado would not confess he even knows

    much less still listens to the Euel Box Quintet
    on "Toddlin'" or "Woodchoppers Ball"   the only regret
    never to have caught them in live performance
    here in this town for that final chance
    since once the trumpet-leader would graduate
    his sax & trombone bass & drums went their separate

    ways to public schools where jazz is seldom heard
    much less played   to some a discouraging word
    few on the road with Herman or Stan or a record date with those
    fewer as first chair with East or West Coast studios
    can only hope wherever they went
    each made music on his chosen instrument

their talents might have been or maybe not
the equal of those of a fellow alum like Giuffre whom none forgot
from here Jimmy had gone to join those idols' bands
to star with Shorty Rogers on Atlantic's *Martians*
Come Back!   his name listed in liner notes
with the likes of a Mingus   his tune set off in quotes

his famous "Four Brothers"   am left now with not even one
dead on the outskirts forever of marriage & the job he'd won
never to share with his bride
a game of golf at the Country Club laid out beside
the Trinity River nor practice on his trap set for another gig
as drummer to roughnecks off an oilfield rig

Letter to Dave Hickey

Today, after a rain,
I was reading your review of
Haley's look at Lyndon
with interest, even
concern as I stepped unsurely here
along our Austin streets.
You'll recall how fond I am
of wandering these ups & downs,
especially when I've had my own.
There's a relief
in corresponding parts,
as you and your wife will attest.
But at any rate
there I was, looking
from the *Observer* to street,
from imagined to imminent
(it's not too far in fact)
when suddenly both were excluded
by the fragrant exudings
of a huge ligustrum.
After that
there were no more politics with,
as you would say,
wettings from the bank—left *or* right.
But tomorrow I'll try to finish
what I started.
O and Dave,
on Sunday
I saw Dobie pass
decked in flowers, and
though I would've felt
out of place (with so many
big shots at the funeral),
I was moved to a pause—could go

no further in thought. That was yesterday,
but always it seems
either the blooming flowers
or the loss of such beautiful minds
as Frank Dobie and Jack Teagarden's
keep me from considering
all the events I know I should.
But in spite of that
you and a few others
still encourage us poets (good *or* bad)
to moon around—Haley included!
For that, our eternal thanks, and
do give my best to Mary Jane.

from *Austin*

San Gabriel

Morton was rooming then across 19th
would share his taste for bottled brew
& for jazz solos from the Golden Age
of Bix's cornet or piano on "In a Mist"
NORK Red Nichols the amazing Miff

"the foursquare same-way-every-time
ragtime feel" of the ODJB's '17 style
Dutrey   Kid Ory   & Vernon's own
trombonists all in a Twenties' tradition
whose licks he imitated to keep it alive

he from Big T's own stomping grounds
& born like Teagarden to travel around
to leave Wichita Falls for eastern roots
though then after a quart he'd introduce
his pride in this place's western twang

at Shakey's Pizza Parlor dixied nights
at 31st & Guadalupe his old-time tone
a straight-ahead drive reviving a need
to play it "For No Reason at All in C"
but to rhythm & rhyme Estevan's city
. . .

George moved his family to Palestine pines
through distance & crisis keeping in touch
roommates ever by the ties that bind
by rockets yet flare & a dog barks on
the errors accepted & the juries hung

a cement holds from that garage apartment

true as well through difference with Andy
patched up by hearing a Scherchen Mahler
listening there together to scherzo & ländler
cutting class for a symphony far more urgent

equally so for Count Basie's "Lil' Darlin'"
atomic album with Lockjaw's tenor screams
detonated over & over off those upstairs walls
when the opening chords on Green's guitar
would set heads straighter than any lecture

Black music for putting a spirit back in
thought History had taken it out of them
by then had surely done its damnedest
yet there they were on & for the record
could enliven not lease a Poplar apartment

at the Co-op found a first Ornette Coleman
on "Congeniality" his white plastic alto sax
as if moaning "I'm Goin' tooo Foat Wuth"
in the Union to catch Bobby Bradford live
those both getting back to Cowtown scales

in between on weekends cleaned up the place
when Andy would prepare a bohemian meal
wine & candlelight imitating a Puccini scene
celebrated a piece written for celeste & strings
bought for the occasion a button-down shirt

would buy one too not to do the laundry
too busy composing to bother with Duz
his ideas brighter the later at night
slept till noon through a major quiz
hoped absence would somehow wash

the important thing to hear new works
professors mostly stick-in-the-muds
had gone on repeating or given it up
above all else would learn that lesson
even to flunk would never succumb

Improvisations on the Notes of Akiko Yamaguchi

May I borrow a pen?
for her palm's a cup
holding her chin,
this whole world's her tiny head:
Guardianess of Mercy
contemplating
would save mankind with
slits for eyes as Ganzin,
Chinese Buddhist, sets sail for
Japanese) shipwrecks,
arrives without sight
(poet Basho,
singing,
sorrows for the loss,
dreams of wiping eyelids with
young leaves from
the "Diary of Saga"
where friends meet again
among the bamboo cane
with solitude & voice of cuckoo
rice wine, small feet
large mind
sit
listening to His thoughts
twelve Generals
become disciples
before the quietest One
as moonlight blew upon 'her
breasts . . . a pair of
golden lotus buds;
the dark points . . . two
blue-black beetles
perched' thereon
and sleep drifted in with

the tide and
out with the pull of
'Māyā . . . life . . .
forever seducing itself'
to the sway of perfumed boughs,
birds 'blasted to ashes
by a glance of her middle eye,'
a laugh that circles the sun,
bows on round straw hats,
'Atomic bomb large experience for
Japanese' paper cranes by
(politely)
Hiroshima patients
make one thousand bring back
happiness
through every street
dragons firecrack
whips snap
the herd turns
to burning sands
or swamp grass
where stands the zebu-cross
Brahma breed
chewing the roots
of an afternoon of
peach ice cream
frozen on the dry back porch
lit by night
by the oil-well torch
and there we were
waitin' on that big spur in the sky
to scourge mesquite
& livid rouge the land
when out of the west

came ridin' on cymbals
of her installment stereo
Andrea's virginal voice
bearin' down
on Lupe's Spanish Village
where Red Garland clomps the
ivories with "I Could Write a Book"
& I could
if only I woodbine
her so-white throat, caress
her every note, and
wade in the paddies
flooded with an old moonlight
Say, José, would you call us a cab?

from "Music History"

The Goodly Company in Chile

At customs they checked for contraband,
uncovered among poetry books the battered horn
I had failed to hock for an engagement ring,
disproving dad's predictive words, though only because
no pitying she had lifted the albatross load.

At my coming flocked by friendly bands;
a bent trumpet there, rare as the mariner's rime;
a place to practice, Atlantis or the Golden Fleece.
For one group a garage was made to serve,
its dirt floor and moss-caked walls

humid even in the glow of the kerosene stove
carried in each time, once the broth and tea had
warmed us up, for Miles' "Someday My Prince Will Come"
and "Green Dolphin Street" or Mingus' "Flamingo,"
gringo greats, though by color I could claim no kin

nor by the way I handled the horn.
And yet it happened even there,
as I hit a note I'd never known,
María and the brothers Echeverría
sensing it too. Later with a less skillful group,

in the room at the head of crumbling stairs,
where fleas leaped about on the circus couch,
to María their act no laughing but a scratching matter,
as we stomped our feet more against the cold
than to make the music go, though even so

as on "Taps Miller" we jammed,
that solid tune from the Basie book,

I felt at last that songless bird slip off.
Even hearing the poor alto imitate Desmond,
the drummer bang & the trombone moan,

& knowing myself a disgrace to jazz,
I suddenly found our ship of fools fully afloat,
my own solo buoyed by the equally bad,
but more by María's backing us all
through the Charybdis of itches & chills.

Pancakes and Prayers

What proof, prove what, or is it just reproof?
The poem that says, despite a D or an F in math,
never making any athletic team, no letter earned,
never running for an olive nor a legislative branch,
I understand, I've come in first, verse is all that counts.

And when it's said to those who fail
yet seek the illuminating flame, no harm is done,
but once it strikes the public eye
through newsprint of *The Daily Sun*,
then fire's no more a metaphor, for the heat is really on.

Out of work, the legal battle gone to court,
I hoe the weeds & trim the shrubs,
then oil & clean my valves & slides
for rehearsal with the Root Beer Rhythm Kings,
for a pancake supper at the Kiwanis Club.

Worley, a redneck from the graveyard shift,
directs the band, taking all the charts by ear
from albums by Ellington or Adderley, whatever jazz

turns up in bins at the Gibson Discount Center.
A screech man once with Kenton, he lets me play the lead.

This night, the tables set with silver & syrup,
the dining hall smoky from cigarettes & sausage,
as family groups file in to eat & we kick the evening off
with "Mercy, Mercy, Mercy," fathers with their heads together,
then turn their cutting looks my way,

indignant that I have shown my face,
after siding with a Black & finding fault
with a local elected man. Then solo on "Satin Doll,"
& I hear Hines say what a job I've done.
No tape survives the date, though plenty of forks & knives.

On Sunday after the minister in protest has left the church,
his wife him, on my account, I rise & lick my chops,
the organ entering first, two bars before my part.
Beginning low, with each ascent and fall
the modal scales reach up & up

to where all doubt would dissipate,
to where the congregation's prayers would hear themselves,
& the self would kiss the soul, without giving in an inch,
were the cotton of politics to be unstopped
by the notes of a heathen's hymn.

Five Versions of the "Twelfth Street Rag"

Euday L. Bowman (1914)

Chording to dad the story goes:
"Euday wrote that rag as a joke.
Sold his rights for a song. Died
'bout as broke
as the player pianos,
the same kind he'd composed it on.
Dust is
all they're good for now. Hanged
if anybody's left to do it justice.
Only the Duke, back in his prime, ever done
it right, the way Euday used to. Why,
old Bowman banged
it out on keyboards missing half the ivories!
Listening to him, drunks would start to cry,
sober fellows turn plain tongue-tied.
Hell, here of late you can't tell where the melody is."

Louis Armstrong & His Hot Seven (1927)

With destinations so unfelt,
faster's now the onliest speed we any know.
After theirs, every session helt

stepped it back up a notch or mo',
but Satchmo's pack yowled it good
'n slow, a howl for the moon, long 'n low.

On piano, no props, no cellophane flood,
Lil, his bucktoothed wife, would sit
goading on those six intense tuxedoed

men, whose field hands of forefathers fit
the battle with hand-me-downs, bent
their backs, & made ready for the chariot.

Fed to the gills on almond juice, grown impatient
with promises sung—lullabied from the cradle up
on work songs, church songs, the chain-gang chant—

some ventured by way the abolition railway. No grail cup,
but quite a drain on the sea of blood, soft-pedaled of late,
& bless me if that ain't trash, for the smallest rup-

ture's worthy of, over cries countless wrongs create,
the thanks of all burdened by this biggest load:
the human bag, shouldered on skins from sun to shade,

slaves to rush, but Hallelu! this rag's rallentandoed.
Heard in a heat, Euday's was scarce a scarecrow bit.
Cut now to a half-time creep, these're fleshin' bones

with tightened nuts, dribble & spit,
stompin' it right on out, & make no mistake,
they're taking root as deep as legit.

What? No castrati, that's Louis' break,
deliberate, a real rip preaching what
no profit ever may, though now-a-days

certain successes is heard to say, "Rot-
gut, let the pious poor, if they choose,
keep their funny proph-

ets, keep their visions too!"
O mute it Gabriel,

listen in Abe, JFK, for this moan moves

majestically on. No whimpering pup with his tail
tucked in, Kid Ory growls it out,
snarls round at heaven's holy rail,

reared to bust right in. Wouldn't though, though doubt
give up. As on one side waxed with that devil Dodds,
even the title's given as plain "Gate Mouth."

There too's another of Papa Dip's miracle rods
tellingly tuned into "Mad Dog" blues,
a rhythm infectious to fish, flesh, flocks,

for pariah, this band's a prick to
any land, a goathead guide, a Virgil
who prods us on, on alone through

the Pass of Fire, blowing it from the wil-
derness, as Moses did, to imaginations
moving on, on to inherit a fertile field

for solemn sound, from true blue guttural friends.

Duke Ellington & His Jungle Band (1931)

Musician of mystery, orchestrator
of African shades, indigo moods;
by voodoo, right off the bat,
he hexes, derails engine to caboose,

duping dancer, listener. Or swinging
a wand-baton flare, a lantern for switches,

he re-voices the very sex of the saxes
to licorice sticks of higher pitches,

uncoupling even Carney's masculine horn
to disguise him Stella, fallen star,
headed straight for Elysian Fields
on board the Stygian diner car:

locomotive the maestro's favorite means
for arriving at Hades unawares—
conductor who never tries putting thought off,
a youngster caught short of the fare,

for he knows he'll hop a ride, hang outside,
at crossings hear us shrill sirens
roaring to whore the unbelieved-in,
woodwinds as alarm there-is-no-fire-in

hopes held unachieved, will see acts of any sort
all pale passengers come to care for,
though true intentions bear a rootless seed,
carry within their why & own wherefore.

Now alternating his brass & reeds
Duke weaves the way to a junction where
blacks & whites can cross the tracks,
where two-piano antiphonals share

the times, cool, toss them forth & back
like hot potatoes or stolen cash:
two years before this take
history records the market crash,

yet song steams mightily on, as Tricky Sam,

oiling it up, a bottle of bootleg beer
halfway up his trombone bell, reels off
Duke's ritual merry-go-round, while Sonny Greer,

fireman he of an imperceptible touch,
keeps on keeping time at boiling,
with Chinese gongs or tin scrub boards,
shoveling a beat as clean as Spring,

a pulsing truth, though ever unuttered,
a sample of Sambo's butter, with strumpets
cooking the feel, stirring up would-be plans
tasty as batter willed undone, trumpets,

with Cootie punctuating among,
now sentencing the soul to speak,
as does an engineering Nanton,
his tongue right in his cheek,

or now again as pepper hot
as Jelly Roll, Juan Tizol
I mean to say, no Don Juan he,
no not at all, but in the role

to season the rag,
outwit keepers of hell's hot ditch,
pen a sneezing staccato fit
on devilish dolls, tricking them into pitch,

for he's an immigrant valve-trombonist,
born & bred a Puerto Rican,
who thumbs his open notes
at pretense, as at Satan—

Jenkins brakes, the band's a flaming expression,
churning & burning till every brass,
out of Malbowges & back on his knees,
whistle stops it, with three short laughs.

Fats Waller & His Rhythm (1935)

Easy as a Pullman porter's shuffle, or so it sounds,
though heaven-bound he is, & faultlessly pounds
it out. What a rag his! that drags us in,
drops a pun, sings weighty what wasn't,
funny bones mid-flight of a ticklish phrase
shouting as if thought painfully sways
away from Swing to a realer rhythm.
Reached by that run, who wouldn't eat a plum,
apple, anything to laugh off the shafts of
this overture that tells, swears no love
ever missed the mark, confides, "Yore shurta find,"
fumbling the heart & humbling the mind.
Weeping clown at the God-box, loader he of dice:
o fine Arabian reader, hear them both & realize
there's less of Variety in Edmund's lay
& upon what Fats would meaningfully play.

Count Basie & His Orchestra featuring Lester Young (1939)

A spare piano intro, Jo Jones on woodblock.
  Basie's left hand a tribute
  to his old Professor Fats, not then mute,
nor ever should be. Let ages rock,
  swing it out for him
  who made of hilarity another hymn.

Not many notes.
  Well-placed instead.
  Here the other day read
where back East in racial riots
  a black business burned
  when wind turned

round, flew fire back.
  Seeing how his dollars done died
  took to suicide.
Rare case that, for black has the knack,
  as any color should, to make it right along,
  to rise up over flapping justice on wings of solid song.

Then leap in, Lester, bend to your life's own tenor,
  hear in that tone your message,
  receive of a reed its minimum wage,
blow it as the last of Swing's big spenders,
  throwing away those hard-earned cents
  to buy by booze a brighter sense.

But where's the end in that? Where's Dickie Wells, trombone ham?
  Humor has served you better than grog.
  You've laughed down every demagogue
'tween Natchez & Little Rock, Texas to Alabam'.
  Euday may have cracked you up, but then you saw,
  as Dada did, how handy a weapon's a good guffaw.

O there it goes, crossing that bridge-like part again,
  that clickity rhythm that eggs me on,
  keeps me hearing this monotone,
this hankering I have on the brain
  for banking on reason's reservoir,
  withering hard rows hoed & prayed for.

O memory's rain, why fall so narrow?
  Soak my road that I may come by feel
    to know how Satch, the Duke, Fats & Bill,
while plowed & replowed under a harrow,
  listened long to the beat of their blood,
    at last to make a music, magic as mud.

Three Haystack Musicians

Thanks to the anonymous namer
from long lost days in junior high
the kid's known now by every drunk from
miles around, as Swingin' Prairie Dog Pete,

drummer nights
at 90 a week, that is to say,
for just how long
not even the leader's in the know.

His honky-tonk side-kick,
the git-tar picker,
stuck right here like the rest of the band,
chords but never once notes

the whereabouts of his fingerboard
for a Cowtown crowd
couldn't care less,
just long as rhythm

& refrain's the same.
And that goes too
for trumpeter Lew,
whose beer-bellied sound

is half-absorbed by his Kotex mute,
who could be gall-durned good,
tootin' that thing while frontin' a band,
or worse in the ears of a sober judge

& then less paid to boot.
But that's just
the chance he'd take
tryin' to make it big on his own,

to play all out,
loud as he would:
the takes? the breaks?
which is the way? Friend this here is

to Debbie's Western Danceland,
single ladies
admitted free
Sundays beginnin' 'round 3:00.

Two Sonnets

epithalamium for Mort

After all the grubby one-night stands,
the eating out alone, aluminum
plates with greasy enchiladas, crum-
my rice, for once you feel like such jazz bands
as find at last a home for Dixielands,
the cool, hot tunes they love, to pack no drums
or bass, or in your case the books of chums
like Ade & Lardner, old forgotten hands
who held you bygone till you felt her warm-
er hold your own. And though unread in novels
ever "cooked" beyond the move you're 'bout to make,
we friends from those shared times know, just as harm-
ony's been half our lonely days, the hovels
rented all were right for us, dis here's a take!

paying dues for Carl

Buzz, the only uncle on my surname side,
whose house smelled of sheet music, "Maple Leaf"
& other rags, has spent these fifteen years
away. Missed nothing since, you see, he knew
no other age than that of straws & two-
toned shoes. A movie. That was when my fears,
his going to the Ladies' for relief
would shame me good, first brought on pangs of pride.
Even now that odor's memory brings them home,
all the tunes I never heard him play,
the suits he spruced up in to Charleston for
a day whose faster trades his First World War,
his 'Twenties mind just wasn't made to stay
up with. You say the rent's due? Here's a pome.

A Wedding Sestina

Everyone inside is dressed up pretty as a picture,
though none of us can manage what the bride
will, without her even trying. White-gloved ushers seat us, as piano
strains set an uninspiring mood, the flowers on the altar
wilting in this warm Southwestern afternoon, when the groom
will do it, four months late. Gathered, all await the vows' repeating.

Up front, the pathetic-but-happy-girl-friend-of-a-pianist goes on repeating
what she was asked to play. An aunt, perhaps, snaps her picture
with Kodak insta-matic. The soloist, some cousin to the bride,
holds her music up, clears her throat, and, askant the altar,
nods three times before the girlfriend at the battered piano
discovers she's ready for her to pour forth song, out upon groom

and congregation, as down the aisle between best men, the handsome groom
ambles to where the singer sings and the aunt stands aiming to take his picture.
Behind the flashing cubes, on this 2nd Baptist Church's bare-walled altar,
a patch of cement crudely glares at us, just as the same piano
piece, begun again, seems, in its unashamed, wrong-note way, repeating
what's awkward here today. And now she bangs an entrance for the bride.

Preceded by a pig-tailed sister and a beaming brother to the bride,
their outfits bright as the building's dull, the mother-to-wed's

    a picture,
her race's, proud despite the crud's been done her, head held
    high, facing the altar
where sex will be approved, her love in need of no repeating.
And smiling in his winning way, dancingly, though quite
    stoned still, the groom
gets set to turn the blues to a "Milenburg Joys" for jazz piano.

With bride and groom joining hands before the sober pastor,
    the pitiful piano
silent now, I see the heavy faces, not this way from a belated
    repeating,
but just because they got here black. How happy yet the
    picture!
For under burdens on their brows, a prideful hope for the
    trembling bride
and her big man breaks out like the grin on a derby winner's
    groom,
as rings like wreaths are slipped on fingers swelling at the
    fanless altar.

With vows exchanged, the sermon at an end, the couple
    descends on altar
steps to the pallid music played again on the out-of-tune
    piano.
But here today harmony has been performed, for this is what
    repeating
is, and so the aunt can run ahead to shoot the sacred picture.
Filing out now with all the rest, I search about for my friend
    the groom,
seated in a black sedan, tied with cans, rice on him and on his
    bride.

Reaching out the window, the groom shakes hands, as we go

    on and on repeating
"Best of luck," "Don't stay up too late," all the cleverness a
    blushing bride
expects to hear. Altar empty, piano shut, baby in another car,
    that's about the picture.

Leaders

Some, they say, are born, others made, at times both.
Inheritor of scepter & servants, Henry the Fifth,
as instance of the third, accepted the throne,
well before his dad's demise, & mounted up,
near Shrewsbury, as monarch he meant to be.

In a rulerless land the same holds true,
for every man, as then, can't ride. Some will
walk behind, some wave as the parade rolls by, yelling
with all their might. In the end each must decide.
Ho Chi Minh circled around, a kind of royal tour:

France, Russia, China, then home again,
where, persistent as a cricket, conscience,
or a faucet drip in the kitchen sink,
his chirp grew out of all proportion,
a Middle Ages cuckoo, that offensive herald of Spring.

With time the writing spread, a Tom Paine tree, advertising
far & wide. Till read as the only way out of the woods,
the old Vietnamese sat on another's nest,
no Ming, but quite a Communist king.
The North invaded, invades the lazy South,

to free the slaves of system.
Moral right their standard then, now it's flown
up-so-doun, for the yoke is what may serve them.
Civil war some say, another piper's all I hear,
for a follower I will ever be, though of any cliff

this cauliflower, this tin ear has been banged wary.
Would yet listen still when Lunceford led, but after him
the band broke up, as every musical mouse crept back
to hole up in remembrance, there to await the beat,

not the whip, not the snap on cheese & head,

but sound ideas instead, how he'd said, "Music is our biz.
Blow it dissonant, brass. Now mute it straight.
Syncopate, string bass. Salute, not me, but variety.
No kowtowing, trombone, just give us the lip!"
Knowing I'm better off backing up another, second fiddle

& all of that, by Christ's bones, given a choice,
Herry Bailly's a vulgar critic, who never knows what's good
from a horse's tail, who swears me yet out of taking Chaucer
overmuch or, what's far worse, so little to heart.
Then too, I could've bowed under a dago, Guido Cantelli,

true son of Toscanini, & of the Italian strain,
conductor who out-feathered the father's magic touch,
floated of an afternoon the faun's loosing flute,
breathed Beethoven's 7th into boundless dance, all
by binding men & instruments with a baton of wood or glass.

The Hero's Fall I Fell For

*or, a poem of the life of
Joseph Oliver (1885-1938)*

Proem:

how have one
"irrelevant"
as Lake Erie receiving a

downpour revolutionaries
Panthers Rudd Che
thick as jungle leaves the

present—while memory can maybe
hack it—keeps on creeping back
its undergrowth so dense with

yells "I'm over here"
light's choked
by every neck of the

woods cleared out by the carload
technologies even weeded by the
peck with loss of now then's a no-
return bottle recovery of

a sense of where
if this is out
that past was heading for
worth the search when one considers

any season's truths
just as tracks have come into the

very valley
shoot enchanted forests right back up

a muse's might help except
all she ever did do
was to see to it the spirit of
kept me on the move movies

vans wings plans
I've had them up to here
would land & get a look
without the legends dating so

takes carbon 14 to find
why a
fork where
was one road

o not another out-
let I'm blocked by countless
routes though what I'm talking 'bout
sounds the same—roots

hear them both but
can't help choose the
blues
& this though every minute

shout
these're the vows
you can't repeat
closed to you whitey stay

out a segregated state

the getting back
"& after all we done
to have them placed real

nice got 'em over here didn't we"
how protest it
drain

my veins
paint
my face

come on minstreling
as Jolson did
with reasons enough

not to arroyos of
drowned guerrillas the
nth degree arguments

programmed-out categorized
apprised by the best
have waded in anyways

through Fortran cards of
innocent blood to an un-
computerized cornet tone

Funky Butt Hall
a history marked
by not much more

happy tragedies
of Joe "King" Oliver

The Hero's Fall I Fell For

American anomaly

died racking eight ball

Mute:

no invention of his own making
introduced it simply
this wanting to be
someone somewhere else

pure pigheadedness
his was
an adornment just
in the sugary hands

of a Clyde McCoy
sounded such
while to the King
a means

of intimation
surely a cap
to stop his beer
from going flat

big bands (Miller *et al*)
blew Joe's "Snag It"
till trumpets in hats
sat on it—a clown act

tin bowlers
that couldn't hide
the fact of

artifice

but when Joe squeezed it in
it left him free to grab us
an epoch away without his running
the customers off

at whose merciless worship
awoke that day to find
himself!   a double favor
one done to sullen ears

wouldn't be disturbed two
the tuning in deserved
three baby makes
caught again O.K.

I'd hear justifyings
for such solo flights
all night long:
the carefuller

touch
the more control
the wa-wa & with Jelly Roll
meowing the alley cat cry

hardships created
specially
such gods as he himself could
go against "pretty good

for a
King of

Spades
wouldn't you say"

Duo:

celibate through the early years
true pioneer till he'd made it big
his only wife his mule-like ways
then sent by mail for a second chair

two cornets to toot the rooftops off!
yet all I seem to come across
is more than men where numbers
rule unlaying roosts

another mouth to feed
the dollars must mount up
& how
population so out of sorts

blessings count them by the gross
or not at all
o what a loss when the thought of alone
can't even stand itself

nor ever will give in an
inch
to sum a schoolboy's
1 + 1

then had he cut him
though Louis never did
& Joe turned jealous just for that
what man goes old without it

Haydn papa of them all
felt the pangs when Ludwig sang
& so it was when Louis split
his only issue

a son who'd been a partner on the throne
o even before his reign ran out
what royalty to have made such room
for a rival certain as Satch

who would come by train
to Lincoln's land of feuding gangs
its northern nights cold as facts
dirty snow hanging on as old Tartuffe

in Louie's southern dreams like candles perfume dipped
white magnolia buds burning unconsumed
but then in blending in
with a brighter horn a surer punch

to out blow even
the Windy City
on to shape
Eldridge & the rest

his notes his
his heritage more
sharing two instead
of just himself

Cotton Club:

Oliver & early Ellington
equally ruling passions
nor in King's nor Duke's own eyes
opponents in any sense but price's

of Louis though before he left
Joe proclaimed
long as he's with me
what's to hurt a King

"then tell us the use
when by that time
ambush
the wrong is out!"

Sultan of the Mardi Gras
parti-colored absolution
another bannered fanfare
one of many paraded to

race it never was an Oliver thing
an Ellington it did become
when Duke called on to take Joe's place
an "unknown" up from the cellars

with his "back to Africa" sound
found that Harlem spot
a very claim
to a sort of sole succession

a 'Sixties' ebony pride
but back then Blacks caught up
in the white demand
for uninhibited primitives

ain't it a bit in retrospect
holding a-cannibal for such a come-down
a simple change in fashion
when the King long had held

his magic name in vain
his fixed amount in mind
& right in the big middle of
the Management's talk

that night in New Orleans came again
same as a sonnet's rhyme
with everyone at the Aberdeens
going on & on about Keppard & Perez:

    How he'd said to George
    Beat it out a solid
    B flat blues
    Strode to the door
    Through so much smoke
    Moistening his lips in summer's evening air
    Aiming his cornet toward Keppard's whore-
    House horn & letting rip with red-hot blasts smithy shoes
    Ringing up to where Perez cooked
    Till out they broke
    Stampeding for Joe the joint in front of which he stood
    Customers crowning him then & there
    His reply to the Club's pre-Depression bid:
    A decline hammered out on that old forge

others say his teeth gave out
pyorrhea got to the gums
but later breaks won't support it

NYC 9/10/28 cut another masterpiece

"Aunt Hagar's Blues"
a Handy tune
no swan song
in that or the year to come

yet some still blame the move
make it a question
of sectional strife
the difference between East

& Midwest life
like a Nixon nomination
& after bitter defeat
his coming out to say

the Senate would never consent
to any Southerner's sitting
Supreme deceit
next to my daily double

any ruse will serve
examples but this from the greatest more
a King courted his holy fame
brings me down as if

& it is
myself I hear
intoning
over & over

Letter to Electra, Texas:

Bunk you oughtn't to waste yourself
I can line you up with plenty good stuff

Don't see the old gang much anymore
That Louis can hit high G with ease

Send me any new tunes you got
I'll get them printed pay you a pretty penny

Write some them low down blues
The kind you always playing

Well I'm doing fine
Tried to get in touch before

But nobody knowed whereabouts you was
Bunk it's your fault you working for nothing

Come on up here to New York
I'd give anything to sit & talk

Bout the old times
Like how Brundy would get me off

While you stealed my music remember
Looking to hear from you real soon

Hope your family having good health
I remain very truly yours   Joe

Spring Death in Savannah:

After the Victor contract dried up
& a Newark agent paid
with a rubber check
my band drifted one by one away

Took another not so good
& headed South
got stuck in the Quaker State
till Sis mailed enough to bail us out

Then the bus broke down
the block cracked from freezing
lost them all & now I'm just
a toothless cornet king

One suit of clothes to my name
can't stand to meet old friends
feel just terrible as hell
the way their eyes take me in

Wrote my niece
hadn't the price of a Xmas card
but wished all the best
to them their bird cat & dog

Sister since the road house close
I haven't hit a note.
But I've got a lot to thank God for.
Look like every time one door close

the Good Lord open another.
Soon as the weather
can fit my clothes

I know I'll do a sight better

Miss the *bright lights* more & more
the life of the damnedest city
saved a dollar sixty in dimes
for a ticket to go & see it

Open the pool rooms at 9 a.m.
and close at 12 midnite
If the money was only ¼ as much as the hours
I'd be all set.

Be ashamed to let myself
be seen
looking this a way
down in New Orleans

Am trying to live near
to the Lord
than ever before
Good night, dear

Martyrs

when the whole crowd's
stoned as on
the Lester Young take

of "Three Little Words"
the sober comes off sounding like
Stephen at the gates

no one listens—
one drunk's even
staggered so near the mike

no one hears
even when he's
brought the album home

or then it works
the other way around
students of late

been staying high / bombed
thru whole college classes
not to learn how not to live

Graduation Day at Stateville Penitentiary

With each visit, we teachers too were always frisked.
Four gates would clang behind us, each secured
before, at the next, a sullen attendant would whip out
a brass-colored key from his leather holster. Escorted,
we came to a large gray barn, the chapel with its well-
kept hedges & lawn, hole & death house adjacent.

Inside, the prison jazz band held it down, ceremonious,
not too loud nor modern for the solemn occasion at hand.
Officials, seated up on stage, looked down on us,
separated from inmates by aisles & uniformed guards,
as only a sense of uncertainty took the edge off
an atmosphere as cold as any I had ever entered.

Knowing hypocrisy their constant charge, I wondered
what it would mean to capped & gowned offenders, but their
entrance lent no hint, expressions blank as the walls they wore.
Black, white, brown, the colors represented. Vo-tech, elementary,
middle, junior, & high, the first two years beyond, guides to
better living, apprentice barber, these the diplomas or degrees,

the good behavior signs they would soon receive.
Watching again, I found their faces unwritten with
reactions to their being there. On record as addicts,
assassins, rapists, they revealed themselves, young & old,
as students decked in commencement robes, though at their feet,
denims showed, those with their numerals stamped in red.

The invocation came as a blow, for the chaplain began:
"Knock, and it shall be opened unto you."
Glancing around, I expected a riot of grins,
but only saw Cohen, a hard case later dropped in Milwaukee
by a sharp-shooter hit him between the eyes, saved his hostage,
his "you know" look taking it all in as any Jew's would.

After the introduction of outstanding guests,
university heads, members of parole & pardon board,
the warden addressed a few of his choice remarks,
a restiveness rippling up & down the rows of folding chairs.
But then their applause went wild, for a young Yale ex,
who wheeled-&-dealed to have a job awaiting.

On coming out, he said, there would be a raise, from 35 to 50.
Cheers like mad. Clearly a "tidy sum" for tempting reformation,
but then I heard him add, they would have to pick it up
on checking in with they knew who. A reference greeted
by a general moan, for he wanted them to touch base first,
before they would do the places & things he left unsaid.

Though feeling, he said, what was most important that day
were the awards for work well done,
he wanted to conclude with a wise man's words,
one who once was challenged by a youth to say
if what he held, were alive or dead. Alive,
the youth would crush the bird; dead, he would let it fly.

To which the sage replied, the answer, my son, is in your hands.
This time the clapping barely audible,
as Yale sat down in an awkward still.
Then came the superintendent of rehabilitation,
who called forward the pen's extension honor graduate,
3.8 from Wright, a Chicago junior college. Serious as ever,

Fisher climbed the stairs. At 23, youngest in my writing class,
a lover of firearms & science fiction, had already served 4 or 5.
For what, I had never asked, over & done. The days drag on,
inside or out. Who wants reminding of the love ungiven
to others or oneself? And then in effect we say,
by the grace of whatever god, he's the one in the cell.

With that the band cranked up a version of Elgar's *Pomp*,
a bit out of tune, since not their style, & yet as the cons went
marching by, I saw the cracks begin, & then they all broke out
with smiles, & the walls came tumbling down, for sheepskins do,
they read reward for portage beyond the bars. O Joliet, o Fox River,
their fingers gave us Vs as proud as captive blood can ever be.

Ornette in Rome

    1.

Following cold months in NYC
    jobless with
love what comes in what goes out having hit

    an all-time low he prospects here
in ruins rich enough to buy
    not oblivion but what

through others' weathered maps restores
    if not the golden melody   for that's
a thing of a

    foreign past   the country touch
the tortuous trail the lost black mine
    of laugh & cry

    2.

like peace tracked down to violent death
    a cooling drink to desert sand
    wholeness is now traced here
    to a back-broken land

    of torsos & shards
    years aqueducts dry
    trees tombs filled still with
triumphs so unknown though memorized

Dave Oliphant

3.

   patched up
     composed
                  for string quartet
   proved
     once & for all
              nobody
   like this one-man band
     could grow up
              to run & win as
   President
     & just before
              inauguration
   the whole
     blamed
              blesséd
   nation
     glued to
              midas TVs
   celebrities
     standing out in
              January snow
   poets
     their laureate lines ready
              tributes to the
   all-American way he rose
     from rhythm & blues
              to the big chair
   where
     Truman's
              buck stops there
   how he
     (heroically) suffered through

```
                        in Baton Rouge
when honkies broke
    his plastic sax
                    'cross his back
& just when
    unmagic words
                    'bout to
solemnize the almightiest show
    would whip
                    a bent trumpet
from his vaudeville tux
    & trade it all
                    for a couple of
electrically
    rapid blasts
                    illogical jewels would
warm
    turn the town
                    to a jillion tears
& weeping a
    belly laugh
                    swear that
sorry boys & girls
    I love you all
                    but have it
kit & caboodle
    cause somewhere in
                    this here
horn
    there's a bigger
                    richer land
to look
    out
                    for
```

from "Nixon"

at the inaugural ball did she dance to forget
bombings & break-ins plumbers & pay-offs
suspecting the leaks weren't plugged for long
a deep throat hole in the dike not a finger fit
or to savor sweet revenge for their '60 loss

at the '69 birthday party she threw for Duke
when for Ellington's 70th in honoring the man
she hosted that royal American at her gala fete
RN swore none swung more stood higher than
can it not draw off the abscess of a dark deceit

& after presenting him the Medal of Freedom
& on his asking him to play for the 200 guests
among them Eckstine Hines Mulligan Brubeck
Cab J.J. Billy Taylor Urbie Green & Desmond
the maestro improvised "Patricia" in tribute to

his First Lady written up as permanent press
not Billy Strayhorn's "Satin" but a plastic doll
every hair in place no substance all small talk
or turn off voters as he drove for higher office
RN saying of her was tougher than finest steel

with the dam bursting poised & self-possessed
as whenever around the house he proved inept
she would stop a dripping faucet unstick a door
slipcover the ratty sofa hang curtains or drapes
my María as well a homemaker extraordinaire

changes the view even more her new red suit
the protesters in Caracas spattered with spittle
dignified & unruffled as it rained from above
at their return he calling for Congress to pass

Exchange bill led to discovery of Chile & her

this town linking their passage by United Fruit
New Orleans to Panama in an oil-smelly hold
to how he failed to take his Starlight's advice
her code name bestowed by the Secret Service
said fit her to a T as it does my María likewise

but mostly before his proposing at Dana Point
to the way she had nursed her mother's cancer
& not long after cared for her father's silicosis
then those in Seton Hospital with tuberculosis
meanwhile in that medical school under Osler

Pat Ireland had observed a colon hypertrophied
catching from "the greatest physician ever lived"
that famed professor's infectious love of history
Sir William's precept on preventive oral hygiene
see it each visit to Latimer to have them cleaned

leading Pat to read & write the medicinal story
of his own home state from Indian plant-lore
to B.E. Hadra's signpost use of a microscope
on his 1874 lesions of vagina & pelvic floor
to TMA rejecting in '52 Negro membership

in '56 as president gave his inaugural address
on how with Cabeza de Vaca all surgery began
his first operation had made him a deified man
with arrowhead he dug from the Indian's chest
at the sacred center of many a festivity & dance

. . .

the doctor-historian's odious name needful too
for learning after Ford had granted him pardon
how Patricia had exploded in asking For what
how after transfusions for hemorrhaging blood
when RN told her he would never pull through

she'd said he had to make it must not give up
in '52 in that critical campaign had said it too
so recovered & later from the threat of a clot
from his phlebitis & bedpans urinals & tubes
measures taken to administer a counter shock

Aitken not holding with a malingering charge
become an invalid & a nearly bankrupt pariah
less indomitable spirits would've lost the will
but with a football philosophy Brennan & her
made his comeback to pass a test of character

at the Great '69 Shootout in the Arkansas hills
(if invasive yet crucial to reassess the rejected)
with Longhorns down to Razorbacks by 14 zip
when they asked at halftime what he predicted
declared Texas would win & by one point did

tough guy riverboat gambler of global twisting
with a Frost interview on TV to prove it again
to reiterate the old phrases had worked before
peace with honor law & order a little break-in
well-intentioned but gave his enemies a sword

believed at last by this the boil had been lanced
then chose Hyden for his first public appearance
small Kentucky town had conveniently planned
to name its swimming pool & a new gymnasium

The Hero's Fall I Fell For   73

for the exiled hero-messiah who had come again

earlier turned down this bears his Nazified name
a '54 invitation to visit here Commencement day
from Mrs. Wheat as sponsor of their senior class
replied "I like small towns   Would feel at home
Needless to say grateful good wishes Sincerely"

& had he come would it have made a difference
could it have cured Gloucester's insomnia curse
the play's best brain from politics of discontent
made him face a corrupt motive the clear intent
of cover-up inconsistency obstruction or worse

have taught him how a cactus can take the heat
will needle yet nourish with pear-shaped fruit
in spite of espinas will quench & still perfume
speak brightly with a yellow aromatic bloom
with refreshing green tongue ever tell the truth

or emptied his medicine chest of Ex-Lax Tums
& Preparation H his mirror's paranoid reflection
did it change Pat Ireland's tune from his in '52
when he wrote to tell RN of the Texas Nixons
"more eager than ever to claim kinship with you"

. . .

had they invited Dr. Lawrence A. a Black instead
such a rhetorical question far too ironic for words
yet see him after winning his Supreme Court case
or three decades later El Paso's transport service
discontinue its colored section without a fanfare

another physician another Nixon yet never to join
the Association as a member from County or State
nor in a Democratic Primary Election to participate
born in 1884 to a Chief Steward on grandad's train
a medical man serving from '09 in the desert sand

first attending Wiley in his hometown of Marshall
founder Rep. Meshach Roberts beaten by the Klan
Mel Tolson debate teams defeating Oxford & USC
then off to Nashville to its Med School at Meharry
three years before Pat I.'s course in Maryland began

one of only two in the nation would accept his kind
paid for training by tending bar & as Pullman porter
from Chi Town to 'Frisco then with diploma in hand
returned to Brazos Valley & there to open a practice
in Cameron where a girl accuses the shoe-shine man

of despoiling her arrested in custody but then dragged
from his cell by a mob burns him in the public square
where Lawrence hears through his locked office door
the dying cries even as from above a balcony crowd
looks on provided for the occasion with extra chairs

. . .

in 1878 Manning honored by Swearingen
his fellow Austin physician for selfless aid
to victims in Mississippi first in Memphis
where for weak & dying a pillar of strength
fearless guiding light till fever extinguished

two years before at the TMA meeting in '76
performing for the cataract in a Negro's eye

a linear incision even as Kirkpatrick deplored
this State operating without any Health Board
urging its protection against all that afflicts

to work together in spite of race or position
while Burt would assert their smaller brain
a lack of vital power & nervous endurance
claimed with disease their lower resistance
less lung capacity Louis' solos all disprove

Professor Douglass Parker Keeps Charlie Live at the Harry Ransom Center

dateline Austin July 24 1986
"Cadence" a local sextet
of lead trombone alto sax guitar
piano bass & drums
is cooking here at the HRC

their first piece "Bebop" by Gillespie
backed up by the Michener Gallery's
pop art on permanent loan
a *Dead Veteran* by Larry Rivers
dressed out in spangled red-white-&-blue
splashed & dripped from top to bottom
Tom Wesselman's drawing for *Still Life No. 42*
with its black-&-white clock stopped forever
at seven-&-a-half past four
& Peter Saul's *Criminal Being Executed*
with its prisoner strapped in an electric chair
as the Donald-Duck-looking guard's caption declares
"You Have to Fry"
like the two eggs sunny side up
with poison stirred in
from a skull-&-cross-boned bottle
for the Frankensteinish figure's
last & final earthly meal
"Crime Does Not Pay"
painted in pastels across his chest

against this backdrop of psychedelic death
the percussionist pounds & the two horns wail
while in Dizzy's own home state
the cattle drop & the crops now fail
from an unrelenting East Coast heat wave
with Illinois farmers shipping bales of hay
to save their counterparts way down South

The Hero's Fall I Fell For

the same as here at this noonday concert
with soloists each in turn
keeping the notes alive wherever born
even charted on a roll of toilet paper
at Camarillo when Charlie took the cure
& with every classic number
Doctor Douglass
    PhD in Latin & Greek
    translator he of Lucretius
    with his own anachronistic version of
    The Wasps by Aristophanes
labels one baroque
introduces another with
an autobiographical anecdote
before unearthing beneath the chords
a buried pop tune like "Embraceable You"
on which Bird based his "Quasimodo"
Miles hid "Indiana" under his "Donna Lee"
then revives their timeless changes
with his own imperfect sliding tones

this his all-white group except for Hope
a vocalist scats on Monk's "Straight, No Chaser"
& now on Rosolino's "Rubberneck"
the Prof is taking a break
jerking his slide fitfully
digging in to come on swinging
an African-American outside in
creating a world of his own
one he's grown obsessive with
    as with his course on parageography
    brands it a form of self-blackmail
    its character from High Thefarie
    his own invented bumbling DPS

short for
Dionysius Simplicissimus Periphrastes
"an absolute neurotic on
the subject of heaven and hell"
who half the time
is undergoing
therapeutic shock
he himself blowing a kind of mixed-up jazz
attacking themes as did that god
in swan's disguise

the pianist stomping the carpet
his fingers sweeping & picking it up
as the guitarist
in his white tank top
so thin his ribs show through
now whelms & electrifies
the bassist running the gamut
from devil's deep blue sea
to outer space Copernican style
when then the sax man cometh
a disc jockey ironic & shy
riffs in reverse in broken English
with each conjugation declines pretense
sends present & future back to the past
while the drummer beats the rap
of a honky jamming Black
all holding on to the Yardbird line
"like a chorus of 24 armadillos"
behind Doc Parker's leading part
in a summing up of the play's revival
for Charlie's theirs & our own dear lives

Three Musicians Perform Their Freedom

each distinct
in attire & instrument
a trio so intent
in spite of the fact
the paraphernalia
in this bookstore espresso café

must needs detract
from the vital statement
they have come to make
as do the clothes & shoes
worn by each or gone without
for these too are taking away

from the ears' attempt to hear
how free they are
or dream to be
the bassist leader
in mod glasses shirt & tie
with close-cropped hair

first bows upon
his four tuned strings
& then with acrobatic fingers
plucks "Isabel's Table Dance" theme
a "planned chaos" Mingus piece
from his *Tijuana Moods* of '57

the drummer with one foot bare
thumps with his bass-drum pedal
as his short-sleeved shirt
with collarless African design
of black & russet diamonds
coordinates with his faded jeans

then kicks with the rest of his kit
his pair of snares & tom tom
his golden Zildjians
delicately hit
with sticks against
their oval rims

while the vocalist's lips
release her notes in sync
with the cymbals & strings
her sounds rising from deep within
up through her throat & out between
her brightly whitened teeth

though her eyes closed
in concentration
yet fidgets with a right-hand ring
not knowing or so it seems
it draws attention
from her wordless tones

as does her dress
a black tight-fitting cocktail style
with spaghetti straps
lower in front than back
angled skirt & cleavage
upstaging the urgent song

even her painted nails
her high-heeled slings
her turquoise necklace
her face with no make-up
along with the whir
of the mocha machine

& behind & to her side
the sinfully delicious gourmet rolls
advertised on the register sign
all compete with the liberation
she & her men would deliver here
to consumer conscious & fashion aware

María's Radio

keeps her company & up to date
entertains her as she cooks & bakes
marathons in advance of weekly meals
each delicious dish will nourish & fill
the curried chicken over a bed of rice
texmati or jasmine with an onion slice
but first skins debones & boils to a froth
for making the base of a tasty natural broth
for homemade soups of her vegetable mix
or of spinach alone so healthful & iron rich

her favorites the local Scot announcer-singer
Ed Miller on "Folkways" & Garrison Keillor's
"Prairie Home Companion" Terry Gross too
with knowns & unknowns she will interview
on "Fresh Air" & "Car Talks"'s philosophical
grease-monkey brothers who at every call
yuk it up as they dispense advice on muf-
fler ignition switch hydraulic lift along with love
together on NPR with "All Things Considered"
whiling away the only hours ever hear her dread
those spent starching & pressing blouses & shirts
will catch but bits & pieces yet it always irks
on just passing through to the "reading room"
where only jazz & classical would ever presume
resent not so much that pathetic Scotch-Gaelic whine
but rather Paul Ray's program of "Twine

Time" worse than Keillor's satirical lives of cowboys
horse-backed megabites in woe-begone voice
for it's Ray returns to mind her teenage years
Sixteen Candles The Great Pretender Tears
on My Pillow Twilight Time or *Party Doll*
when on slow numbers she will still recall

how Jaime invited her great dancer bigger tease
since his parents permitted no Gentile steadies
see her rocking in his arms around the clock
to *Itsy Bitsy Teenie Weenie Yellow Polka Dot
Bikini It's My Party Little Darling Only You*
till the green-eyed beast again breaks through
almost prefer at seventeen she *had* become
as she vowed she would a noiseless nun
no longer to judge a date by socks he wore
how well he could clutch or in soccer score

though not there in those days only later met
she already twenty-two & knew she was get-
ting a gringo stepped on toes & couldn't sing
couldn't stand his own forebears' Highland fling
a Texan given to the darkest of Irish moods
not half so smart nor clever as all those Jews
she's ever admired & yet will share the shows
that I may learn through her of trumpet solos
by Marvin "Hannibal" Peterson of Smithville
then ride in our son's Fairmont cherry mobile
to San Antone & hear with him that live quartet
perform with the city orchestra *African Portraits*
will insist that I hurry out of the gloom & listen
to Billy Taylor analyze on "Morning Edition"
Strayhorn's *Lush Life* with its amazing changes
such progressive harmonies as she too arranges

On Visiting NYC

become just another
winter leaf covers
pavement instead of

earth one more
flake upon the
piles of snow

each a pattern
all its own
till sun's thaw

turns the sodden
leaves to a
soggy mass &

melting sweeps the
huddled decay into
the East River's

shimmer underneath Hart's
harp-like Brooklyn Bridge
to which he

limned lines forever
linked to tuned
cables lift cabbies'

fares crossing over
as the ferry
did when the

current hastened with
Walt's well-joined disparate

crowds descending now

in jets whose
wing tips blink
their warning lights

as myriad stars
wink at the
avenues lit with

welcome as do
the runways at
LaGuardia & JFK

as Liberty's torch
shines brightly still
for her multitudinous

poor in sight
of Shea where
immigrants play for

exorbitant pay as
oil sheiks in
flowing robes pass

through Customs with
bearded kippahed Zionists
wearing fringed prayer

shawls all so
eager to turn
their laptops on

a movie crew
from the down-under
land of koala

& kangaroo here
perhaps to reshoot
Mighty Joe Young's

attempted escape from
the asphalt cage
to climb again

the Empire State's
injection needle a
plane's decaled fuselage

reading "Bombardier" recalling
London aflame from
Luftwaffe bays' incendiaries

then later the
getting even over
Dresden's flak-filled skies

while here Twin
Towers missing from
those prefer to

die for an
evanescent heaven than
live for the

sacred real till
fearful now which

edifice or place

next in line
o not you
Grand Central Station

your hopeful throngs
meeting trains with
open arms or

bidding fond farewells
o not you
dear Central Park

with your scads
of skaters &
your lone unknown

jazzer with his
familiar tones his
empty saxophone case

awaiting strangers' hands
may drop no
bomb but bill

or coin near
ponds with geese
preen on solid

rock holds up
skyscrapers the subway
riders just arriving

natives rarely leaving
belonging forming as
poets have written

a part of
your famed Indian
Dutch anonymous scene

Jazz by the Boulevard

for Donna Van Ness

    yesterday
    on a temporary
    outdoor stage
    the Heritage
    named
    for the Park Cities Bank
    in recognition of & to honor
    this festival's money-lending sponsor
    Marchel Ivery performed at 69
    & today on the Coors Light Main
    David "Fathead" Newman at 74
    is holding forth
    Marchel having honked & swung on
    "Star Eyes" "Bag's Groove" & "Lover Man"
    now David does the same in & on "Hard Times"
    & also Hoagy's "Georgia on My Mind"
    having opened with "Billie's Bounce"
    as whites blacks yellows & browns of Cowtown's
    crowd mill around or in portable seats
    shake heads & tap their feet to the quartet's driving beat
    beyond the shadow of Will Rogers' Memorial Coliseum
    across from the Kimbell Art Museum
    here for this "cowboy & culture" promotional scheme
    a city manager's dream
    to celebrate the Lone Star's native sons
    to generate a few jobs & a bit of income
    for local citizens most in shorts
    & the majority sports
    a pair of shades from the sun's late September blaze
    as even in these autumn days
    it just keeps burning on
    bright & unseasonably strong

with a little of the force
of these Texas tenors
blowing yet with might & main
despite age's unrelenting aches & pains
rhythm-a-ning or improvising a blues
or on pop tunes of Tin Pan Jews
bringing joy to all have come to hear
who never knew a Ku Klux fear
here one block over from Camp Bowie
the brick-paved street intersects with University
where the admission is gratis
thanks to Cadillac's
major financial grant & to volunteers
manning booths include that Rocky Mountain beer's
causes one to wonder does hurt & happiness accord
with the roots of a minor chord
can the melodic blend in any song
set right a lingering wrong
seems so to go by the loving-it look
when these Black men cook
with their hard-bop licks
their soulful stratospherics
a look apparent on every listener's face
regardless of race
or place of birth
due in part to an elegant auto's corporate worth
but more to elder statesmen hanging on
to produce a dateless priceless tone

from "Community Music Fest"

: *New Orleans Jazz Band*

their retiree quintet at this
third annual Austin event
brings alive a city missed
even by those have never

witnessed its Fat Tuesday
or its French Quarter café
whose name gave birth to
"Tin Roof Blues" their re-

vivaled version not their best
since short tonight their clari-
netist busy with a real-estate
deal & yet the notes blown &

banjoed render a tradition known
'round the globe heard here now
as they all come marching in to
"That's a Plenty" a barn burner

features the cornetist who started
on his horn at the 6th-grade center
later joined IBM his embouchure
in boyish shape as he rips rings &

hits high C right on the money
as did before him legendary Bix
more for love of it than any tips
the trombonist too with his instru-

ment a valve-slide combination
for other gigs wails on his mean

bass trumpet a Bach Stradivarius
the same brand as Cy Touff blew

in Herman's 1950s' Herd & with
Richie Kamuca on his tenor sax
in that West Coast style of jazz
but can tell this is Dixieland by

the old guy's washboard-cowbell-
cymbal all rolled into one his feet
dancing as fingers drive the beat
while the tuba player with on his

shoulder his helicon "the hell you
say" pumps away as in those slow
parades to the Crescent City grave
on the way back swinging out with

"O Didn't He Fly" the ghost flown
to join as mourners then believed &
some still do a heavenly host'll sing
as Louie did when soul comes home

Boat House Grill

on Friday nights
it features "Yo
Gadjo" Slim Richey's

trio at its
family-style gravel-floored venue
with two holes

in its corrugated
roof live oaks
grow up through

while from its
ceiling hangs an
entire canoe &

near it a
fake netted trout
a taxidermic real

on the entrance
wall & on
its north a

trophy next to
oars & life
preservers with outdoor

motors leaning along
a facing wooden
ledge beside a

stage of planks
barely raised with

on it amps

mikes & the
instruments already tuned
for couples below

sit on green
picnic benches have
come to eat

to Western Swing
the food as
ever catfish burgers

& fries &
corn dogs for
all the kids

for the grown-ups
young & old
bock Shiner beers

sipped as now
Django Porter in
his black-&-gray toboggan

begins to twang
Reinhardt's "Swing 42"
his Gypsy namesake's

Hot Club piece
from World War
Two in tandem

with his leader
who's all decked
out in blue-jean

pants Hawaiian shirt
black white-banded hat
matching two-toned shoes

his white wispy
beard reaching not
quite down to

his palm-treed shirt
as he strums
chords & peers

at the shaking
heads through his
glitter-rimmed woman's glasses

& now on
all five strings
he rings out

"It Don't Mean
a Thing If
It Ain't Got

That Swing" then
follows it with
"There Will Never

Be Another You"
as Francie Meaux

Jeaux his barefoot

mate keeps the
beat on upright
bass while letting

out a jubilant
yell as the
clientele pat their

feet on pebbles
from creek bottom
or stream-fed lake

their children breaking
into delighted dance
when then with

the grateful tips
their parents have
sent they drop

them into the
minnow bucket of
this fisherman's dream

Serenading the Neighbors

when younger I would leave the window open
that those might hear jazz or classical I played
not sounds of my own but records others made
certain hearing them they would love them too

if any heard none either complained or praised
in later years I would leave the window closed
even on nights without the air-conditioning on
once I could see how presumptuous I had been

& then last week I recalled that arrogant youth
when down the street a brass quintet rehearsed
within the leader's garage with the door left up
the whole block having to hear the instruments

whether we wanted to or not but o I did indeed
walking there to be closer to the glorious notes
I watched listened & applauded for every piece
as those had not for a music I'd forced on them

Part Two:
from *KD: a Jazz Biography*

Vikings in Reverse

did biblical Ham ever come near
in the prince's mind a prison cell
but for the Texas bop trumpeteer
Denmark meant was treated well

from live tapings in Copenhagen
at the Montmartre Jazzhus in '63
hear *Short Story* KD's hardy CD
bears his name in black on green

its title tune taken Sheridan says
in part from "Tickletoe" by Prez
or a "head" remembered by Ken
& his four all-European sidemen

but doesn't include Rolf Ericson
whose trumpet *is* on another CD
from that land of a midnight sun
K's *Scandia Skies* it too from '63

December 5th his other from 19th
with title tune to render tribute to
being in cold so warmly received
by that city & by its music venue

"It Could Happen to You" a hall-
mark solo by each then RE alone
on Bonfá's "Manhã de Carnaval"
its bossa nova Ken'd heard in '61

& on *Short Story* that same piece
but there it's a southwestern tone
with K probing at his loping pace
& "São Paulo" K's entitled home

of prodigious João Carlos Martins
pianist who recorded all of Bach's
preludes gigues fugues & gavottes
corrente notes as if fins in streams

just as Kenny too can fish-like zig
& zag leap flash & the current dig
but would not've caught João live
yet Brazil in *Una más* reissue '95

floats there on Lerner & Loewe's
"If Ever I Would Leave You" o's
slowed until they're "bittersweet"
when K subtly trills its bossa beat

by the '90s Arthur Moreira Lima
reviving Ernesto Nazareth in Rio
he whose "Travesso" can seem a
Schubert ländler Joplin rag-tango

recalls in '94 on her wedding day
Elisa's paying for Russell to play
to lilt EN's "Confidências" at Inn
on the Creek to where was driven

by Milo dreamed-of carriage ride
from chapel to reception as bride
to her Brazilian groom their cake
shared decades after KD to make

his Danish dates unheard till '93
on Nils Winther's SteepleChase
the Bird's tune he chose to base
his label on in Parker's memory

Nils' forebears who'd never cut
nor mixed a disc but adzed long
serpented ships flexible enough
to take the waves & never bang

smooth & sleek as they cleaved
a sea & K notes sailed the same
through his lanky Texian frame
his melodiousness light beneath

an overcast sky as Scandinavian
as Rolf's last & illustrious name
through it perhaps Rolf even kin
to the one named new lands Vin

Leif the Lucky discoverer from
the end of that first millennium
on bass it's a prodigy at just 17
Niels-Henning Ørsted Pedersen

whose line's more likely related
to the marauders of monasteries
to Kiev founders told the stories
of Sigurd Fafnirsbane was fated

to slay a dragon drink her blood
& from it draw the secret words
uttered in conversing with birds
whose sense but she understood

a mocker Kenny's sort of singer
whose tones rarely if ever linger
its rhythms & refrains inventive
hardly repeating so imaginative

The Hero's Fall I Fell For

unstuck on a monotonous pitch
a bobwhite's two-toned whistle
or the grackle's ignition switch
K & the mocker more variable

the CD insert photo a close-up
of his dark pin-striped suit hair
& skin contrasting with a glare
from white shirt-collar & cuffs

his valve caps under fingertips
his horn's mouthpiece pressed
against the all-but-unseen lips
head tilted down toward Alex

Riel's upward slanted cymbal
forming a sort of halo behind
Kenny's slightly angled hand
as third finger pushes middle

valve halfway down for mel-
ancholy with tongue aflutter
flatting a 5th in a major scale
for blue minor never despair

but how ever in frozen fjords
if on a Brazos farm scorched
by mid-July what skaldic age
knew such southwest passage

not even metaphysical Donne
K coming to find & take com-
fort in Spain's Tete Montoliu
in the Allan Botschinsky flue-

gelhorn & in his mix of Danes
& Swedes & with Norwegians
January '64 at Oslo Metropole
issued on '92 Landscape label

but his descent there different
from Miles on J.J.'s "Lament"
K pouring down as a waterfall
cataracting into unfathomable

depths ascending to intensities
buoyed by rippling liquid keys
as Tore Sannes softly tremolos
to heighten KD's soaring solos

another Pedersen on bass Björn
his given name & a Christensen
Jon joining on drums to explore
that heart of darkness continent

with this seer of northern lights
who had ancestors been unsold
unshipped in a perdition's hold
chanting tribal rhythmical rites

unground by subjugation's mill
not tilled their New World field
had never known blues' mystery
had never failed in his chemistry

his physics either or on the road
come to hear with Isaac-Newton
ears an equal & counter reaction
rocket's red flare blast & payload

The Hero's Fall I Fell For

as if taking lessons from Viking 8
or any flight with all of its weight
a strewn wreckage if its fiery hull
unlifting from a gravitational pull

though Ken would learn it through
a Poppa Dip who had broken loose
Bohr too with his quantum theories
hydrogen lines in a spectrum series

with light emitted inside his reactor
as its slow neutron or divided atom
leaped away at angular momentum
Niels depicts in a kitchen metaphor

of the simple tap with its water drip
its fission as in a trumpeter's falling
from his long glissando to split a lip
Bohr's earlier work Einstein calling

a kind of music of the highest form
father of A bomb but first to charm
all those within his realm of thought
to sail for Baltic ports & if K caught

a plane instead not for any theorem
but proof of an energy in every beat
for if in physics Ken never received
any passing grade was still to blend

a science of sound with an alchemy
for radiating electrical orbital notes
Niels' own at risk from Nazi shoats
both wavelength & starred ancestry

but aided by those crafty Norsemen
whose descendants too abetted Ken
lettered their intrepid sagas as runes
the Greek & Latin etched on stones

riveted planks for the rugged firth
floated as would K from bar to bar
each formed by his Post Oak birth
by Austin & Marshall prior to war

later tempered in Oakland & NYC
put through bop's exams by Dizzy
& Bird & by Fats' red freezing ice
by Eckstine's band & later Horace

Art & KD first Messengers to deliv-
er the word & then in '56 Ken with
his Prophets spreading it too as J.R.
Monterose on tenor'd peck in order

now here composes for blonde blue-
eyed scions of rovers' coastal pillage
Thor obeyed on whale road & slough
though KD's trip required no portage

no dragging of keels nor a battle gear
no barter goods hauled from Dnieper
down to Byzantium rather his arrival
come by a school separate & unequal

where they jeered at a blow-boy sissy
where at recess its playground's bully
in wait for dishing out a daily socking
& in self-defense he'd take up boxing

& on receiving Draft Board greetings
sparred a bit but handed best beatings
by Gillespie pugilistic big-band brass
punched it out taking licks sitting last

but held his own with a Navarro & Stitt
in separate late-summer sessions of '46
yet wasn't to go the full bruising round
as did in Dallas both Handy & Garland

in a then smoke-filled Deep Ellum ring
duked it out for ten neither taking dives
later to lay down chords but in winning
at the bell just belted by Golden Gloves

lacing them on with their knuckles sore
then hung them up for those studio gigs
for the solos after they'd signed up with
Miles or Mingus & then a battling more

with a needle's allure the deeper release
promise of nuanced tone a locked-hands
sonic boom Kenny too to know its tease
but his a higher flying over Greenland's

arctic arm & the island Danes possessed
their Faroe & as well Brahe's Uraniborg
where for science's sake Tyco impressed
his peasants for the constellation formed

above Ken's boyhood home later to fear
going up on stage with a Diz or Brownie
the Extra headline shouted for all to hear
"Superstar Fades KD a Fallen Luminary"

but not giving up K simply never would
from his lungs to every lymphatic gland
would dedicate all to give-&-take could
count him in & on him to play his hand

just passing then over Kronborg Castle
by way of Elsinore & a sound-toll fund
Tyco collected for erecting his celestial
globe to track the galaxies gyre around

& for his prediction of the conjunction
of Mars with the Moon in Orion's foot
could fix the comet's parallax position
to send such findings from his Institute

as through his press he'd publish word
of stellar harmony as on any LP record
K had made not to align a special view
nothing in his cosmos so Yardbird new

nor offered supernova leaping forward
to swing on axis of the musical spheres
never claimed to be as Tyco did a Lord
of any sky whose egocentricity appears

in his Urania elegy with a praise of will
of soul conceived as the unforced mind
its declaring few could manage to bend
the stars to their own rule as he in exile

& yet though he'd notate sightings right
Kepler would find all his ellipses wrong
would it ever apply in the world of song
Ptolemy out of tune in the Tunisia night

if Ken toured Ty's mural & his azimuth
saw quadrants ponds & fountain sluices
caught their geometrical design or from
hidden tubes the concordant microcosm

he might've flipped but on "Our Thing"
did K in '63 half think or intend to bring
seasonal winds together the hot cold wet
& dry to form some black hipper Hamlet

or ever see himself as Beowulf taking on
a Grendel in a test of bare-fisted strength
famed branded banned moors-fen demon
whose blood thirst a thane had quenched

& to turn thereby into the Heorot savior
to quaff honey mead with its ring-giver
or to K.O. as Brown Bomber did in '38
the Führer's own pure super Aryan race

or outrun the field as did a Jesse Owens
threw in Hitler's plan a monkey wrench
when with four golds sprinter had nixed
Adolf's grand '36 propaganda Olympics

or decry in ten acts as did from his pulpit
a Kaj Munk that clergyman & playwright
who braved Herod's iron-cross swastikas
till they'd drag his corpse through ditches

instead of those K & Co arranging a head
rendered as their soulful hard-bop version
of Lester's '40 riff on Basie's famous side
with tenor Buddy Tate KD's fellow Texan

waxed the same year fabled Valaida Snow
the Chattanooga singer & Trumpet Queen
had been she would say interned by Dan-
ish police thank goodness not by Gestapo

on July 26 recorded her "St. Louis Blues"
with their local band of Winstrup Olesen
black star decked out in a pale orchid suit
dazzled with her vocal jive & biting tone

reminder now of Prez's '45 "DB Blues"
titled on being stationed & remanded to
the detention barracks on facing another
trumped up charge of a Jim Crow Major

who found in digging into his footlocker
Prez's white wife's photograph & main-
tained his pills illegal those a G.I. doctor
prescribed for severe rectal surgery pain

Val detained in a Danish camp up to '42
kept away from decadent Scandinavians
thrived on jazz even the SS sneaked it in
Danes crossing over to Skåne 7000 Jews

had saved David stars with private boats
& in '39 gave welcome to a jazz royalty
the Duke & his Orchestra's indigo notes
still reigning in ears with love & loyalty

& the leader & his men knew them true
for on "Jack the Bear" the Blanton bass
remains inspired propelled by the place
"Serenade to Sweden" pays homage to

with Ellington at his piano so subdued
it makes it so trumpeter Wallace Jones
must whisper softly with flowery mute
to Lawrence Brown's subtle trombone

then Carney on his nonpareil baritone
reaches into the reed's supernal range
to anchor & preserve those drift alone
on emotion's waves wreck or estrange

in '50 Bird would arrive in Stockholm
to a Bromma airport crowd so welcom-
ing it astonished him while he for Lars
Werner *the* experience of all his years

forever moved by the concert & a jam
session later at Helsingborg when sax-
ophonist improvised with a deep relax-
ing feel on "Star Eyes" & too on "Em-

braceable You" though "Body & Soul"
not up to that amazing rendition of '42
in part from the drummer's over intru-
sive kit or perhaps with Parker too full

of Swedish schnapps not yet that tune
would record with Red Rodney in '51
but that gin drink he gave it as its title
after the visit to Lars so unforgettable

as it must've been for any who heard
& were touched by the genius of Bird
& surely again in '53 when a Clifford
Brown'd arrive in their land to record

with Swedish All-Stars Quincy Jones'
"Stockholm Sweetnin'" would amaze
with his solid trumpet sound & phras-
ing rich in stimulating luxurious tones

& even before his chorus a reliable Art
Farmer no slouch at all shared the solo
space with his own fine showing smart
unflamboyant a morsel tasty & mellow

& again in '61 Lars with Bertil Sundin
asserting Monk in Stockholm had been
among their very greatest moments yet
album out of print only burnt duplicate

Lon Armstrong made attesting to an *Or-
kester Journalen* review wherein Bertil
wrote of that High Priest-Rouse perfor-
mance "swung so could hardly sit still"

in "I'm Getting Sentimental Over You"
pianist's dramatic timing's so unerring
his scalar runs as ever surprising anew
tenor infectious if not quite so stirring

in '58 the Dave Brubeck Quartet came
to delight the Danes on doing that tune
from Danny Kaye's movie done in '52
based on Anderson of a fairy tale fame

hear now the audience clapping in time
to their own "Wonderful Copenhagen"
with Paul Desmond's dancing alto ring
while Dave's waltzing its happy theme

in '59 the Gillespie Quintet in concert
showcased Leo Wright on alto & flute
his lightning runs & his thunder burst
one other fellow Texan so overlooked

in '60 an MJQ "Django" in Göteborg
with its majestic Jackson mallet work
celebrating burnt-fingered Reinhardt
rang with two digits his gypsy guitar

Heath's ostinato bass pumping it out
& Kay's always tasteful cymbal fills
press as Lewis' piano gingerly builds
to his blues-striding whispered shout

each member of the sound ensemble
making music from his heart & soul
each recognized by his touch & tone
on the instrument had made his own

in following year Basie with a palm
for joy spread to Swedish hinterland
towns Malmö & Borgholm on Öland
isle & in Varnamo before Stockholm

concerts at Gröna Lund where Ake
Persson sat in on "Blues Backstage"
& the Swede took a gutbucket page
out of Ory for a hip trombone break

& Texan Henry Coker answered on
an arrangement of "In a Mellotone"
with his stylish 'bone & on trumpet
Fip Ricard a ball in "Corner Pocket"

in '61 too Eric Dolphy with Danes
Erik Moseholm on bass Bent Axen
keyboard & Jorn Elniff percussion
jam-packing Studenterforeningens

the Copenhagen lecture hall where
after "The Way You Look Tonight"
after Eric's bop tags so out of sight
unison applause calls for an encore

then renders "Laura" with allusion
to "Pop Goes the Weasel" not only
proves the relativity of either's key
but a free jazz meaning serious fun

from lands old & new light or dark
old-time hits fit for the avant-garde
quotation of Mother Goose rhymes
an Ornette Tchaikovsky lick in '59

after it in '65 to rouse a Stockholm
with his raucous alto right at home
to let "Snowflakes & Sunshine" in
on his self-taught trumpet & violin

for "Riddle" & "Antiques" joined
by David Izenzon's classical bass
Charles Moffett's drums roof-rais-
ing or bell soft on "Morning Song"

a sequencing termed "pure beauty"
his optimism not alone the Swede
received at its Golden Circle duty
free but filling every crying need

then for '64 Albert Ayler Quartet
with pixy Cherry pocket trumpet
turning on on *Copenhagen Tapes*
following in Coleman's footsteps

in his boyish voice Albert himself
recalls in high school oboe & golf
says in Scandinavia feels truly free
one day U.S. to be as it ought to be

"Children" with its whines & yells
pitches the typical temper tantrum
"Mothers" outlandish romanticism
"Saints" quote recalls the spirituals

"Vibrations" fitting of crisis to a T
as Gary plucks & on drums Sunny
wails converting pop Swedish folk-
songs to their "Spirits" & "Ghosts"

no language Kenny spoke but who
knows he might have learned it too
yet not K's shtick neither exorcism
nor rage *his* a calid holistic tongue

as the Hans "Hornbook" alphabet's
open to both sides secular & sacred
closes the generational gap with its
troop of signs'll rout a white or red

so much depends either glad or sad
upon the letter order written or said
with D in Denmark his bonnie land
God shield it in His protective hand

C for Columbus at Amerigo's shore
turning a world twice its size before
while KD's book just flats & sharps
no verbal notes & no nautical charts

yet Ken to out sail even Christopher
since along with travel transatlantic
on his "Bombay" & "Lotus Flower"
he'd cover seas the Admiral missed

& if K's Half Note "Jong Fu" of '66
came in wake of such oriental motifs
as Fletcher Henderson's '24 "Shang-
hai Shuffle" '28 Ben Pollack "Sing-

apore Sorrows" & in between Louie
with a killer '26 "Cornet Chop Suey"
in '31 "China Boy" of Fats & Big T
& in '40 Cab's "Chop Chop Charlie

Chan" yet still K'd map in "Mexico
City" "Tahitian Suite" "São Paulo"
& "Monaco" cosmographies Brahe
with all his scopes could never see

& if K borrowed had not a Brahms
& for sound tracks to western films
most out of Copland's *Billy the Kid*
on which changes has jazz not lived

with "Prince Albert" he would seize
the day from Kern's rich harmonies
in "All the Things You Are" & then
partly to pattern "DX" on Gershwin

"I Got Rhythm" taken in every way
& "Don't Explain" a Billie Holiday
U stands for Uppsala a stately town
find on the globe its name set down

northwest of "Dear Old Stockholm"
where its folk tune Getz would hear
or must assume since cannot phone
to ask Meehan so admired his tenor

the Davis '56 Quintet cut it for sure
where Red feeds 'Trane the chords
for his o there aren't enough words
not even Hans' can hope to capture

though maybe in "Golden Treasure"
where his drummer boy is off to war
the father's proud the mother fearful
both the tale & explication an earful

but lacks the All-American Rhythm
that section of Paul Chambers' bass
Philly Joe's sticks & Garland states
so elegantly Miles's Scandia theme

after Satchelmouth had set the pace
with a '24 solo on Henderson's side
of a tune of Indiana's Charlie Davis
so curious how he'd come to decide

on "Copenhagen" a title's abstruse
mysterious in origin unlike a blues
or the Savannah-born "Yamekraw"
of James P. Johnson striding Paw

Dipper's maybe is more complex
than one of the Wolverines & Bix
whose dah-dotdotdot of May 26th
to reverse no victory of Ludwig's

nor to send a message of distress
theirs a reply to fog-bound ships
& if Morse's code is now retired
such a short-long sound inspired

the Mahler *Fifth* can ever rescue
by its rhythmic numerical magic
in its trumpet's 4-note call & too
any blown by Bunk Beiderbecke

or Ken with his counter-reacting
style of running like Jesse's stole
the show & if K had won no poll
to Blakey still the crownless king

yet K content being one of many
to add to the others his *quiet* part
lend a little to the horns of plenty
to make it more a matter of heart

O-Yo-De-Lay-Hee-Hoing

on his two-year-old a satin-black
with forehead mark a whitish dot
a bridle Sears & Roebuck bought
he'd drive dogies to a dipping vat

aspiring to cords for alpine vocal
harmonizing vowels as cowhand
not with any falsetto of perpetual
boyhood no castrato's half a man

but a joy in yodeling of every age
from the African pygmy Austrian
Rumanian Swiss & Scandinavian
to campfires out in cactus & sage

hankered to warble as all the men
pictured singing on a silver screen
back then just the Gene Autry sort
no Pickens ever in a Republic part

closest thing to an improvised ride
mockingbird's 50 calls so accused
of copying squeaky gates any type
of peep its repertoire badly abused

while in Witter's Grenstone poems
he's declared the pilfering of tones
creates a medley out of a multitude
a single song hatched from a brood

while a chachalaca'll stick to "staccato cadence" a mocker will "chirp whistle stutter & yodel" as buzzard wheels with just a silent dip & tack

could recognize a mellifluous dove
woodpecker's tap on a hollow trunk
learned each sound as any Audubon
a Longoria with his brushlands love

hearing her choir do "Precious Lord"
that joyful noise at Sunday's service
always choked up Alfreda Inglehart
K too attended the sanctified church

its swaying congregation patting feet
clapping hands in humid August heat
to hymns soldiering onward in Christ
in the *Elmer Gantry* film its cornetist

leads choir helped André Previn win
an Oscar for his lofty score & on *My
Fair Lady* a hard swinger as he'd fly
across his keys to drum-bass Friends

but traded jazz piano for a London
gig of Rachmaninoff works as con-
ductor of Sergei's *Symphony No. 3
Isle of the Dead* a "*Crag*" Fantasy

that '60 movie based on just a sole
Sinclair Lewis episode a repetitive
plot about its likable but seductive
preacher Lancaster in Elmer's role

but largely changed from the novel
like Sister Sharon played by pretty
Jean Simmons quitting the revival
or she says she will & even marry

The Hero's Fall I Fell For

yet persisting tent catches fire with
her inside Burt forgiving panicked
knocked her down rushing to save
sinful lives over which she prayed

when K's Pop would speak of God
he couldn't accept poor being good
if wealthy gained from fruits of evil
a heavenly hope made life tolerable

here on earth but said unworthwhile
lost religion found it all too political
compared it to booking agent who's
out for self not for sake of the muse

but's getting ahead has first to touch
his Sis Eva Lois' keyboard on which
she learned pieces attending Lincoln
High in Palestine played for bottling

companies for a Dr. Pepper in Waco
for Coca-Cola its weekly hour show
to promote its drink with a selection
of sight-read tunes Handy Ellington

she to prophesy K's always jumpin'
up & down to her music must mean
would grow up a Louis or a Gabriel
bright biblical high-toned archangel

K's "Mack the Knife" of '59 his own
rocking take on song of Weill-Brecht
the piece Papa Dip did with his direct
& unembellished New Orleanian tone

but before bop coming sharecrop bail-
ing of hay & alfalfa pulling boles scal-
ing & weighing of sacks twice as long
as K & the boiling of cane to sorghum

herding a hundred head to local corral
begging handout for that peg-leg hobo
bound for Frisco spied oil lamp's glow
tested first by his Mom forever cordial

& from white bum's yarns his yearning
to ride the rods to the Mexicans' border
envisioning maybe Henrik Ibsen's *Peer
Gynt* from "Hall of the Mountain King"

if he listened to Grieg's incidental Suite
his ears in school skied dizzying slopes
of Norway's Gjendin ridge its ice floes
reindeer crackt with Peer in hot pursuit

on "Minor's Holiday" Ken hanging on
to Anitra's theme as if some folksinger
hopped a freight & swung by its ladder
with rails clicked him to a distant town

& after he'd watch the V-shaped flocks
honking high overhead as the Sunshine
Special blew lonesome 'cross its tracks
he'd find a Bull Durham roll-your-own

a tramp's butt to be smoked on the sly
since no tobacco at home no one drank
only watermelon under a star-filled sky
as bullfrogs sang to an ice-cream crank

The Hero's Fall I Fell For

soaking up & absorbing nature's music
began with the rooster's morning crow
from their mud hole the grunt of a sow
with nightfall growls croaks & crickets

in spring a mateless mocker urging on
the one out there with a singing meant
for her alone outlined by a risen moon
his lyricsless call "This Is the Moment"

in '58 K's rendition of Robin's words
in the same year his "Where Are You"
from that team of Adamson-McHugh
but had known their songs from birds

living six miles out had rarely bought
Fairfield paper as vagabonds brought
earlier news of Rangers busting a still
remembered chasing of a Villa a Dill-

inger & a Baby Face read special bul-
letins of the poem on Bonnie & Clyde
written in her blood before she'd died
of 10 G-men dead in Big D gun battle

knew a nearer death in old board well
from when a curious cat had fallen in
as the bucket rose so would the smell
with their water rotten dug a new one

knew too the windmill's metal clang
lifted precious liquid from far below
with curved fan blades turning sang
a pumping song made the cattle low

knew the ubiquitous plains machine
with self-governed centrifugal force
saved in drought cow sheep & horse
kept okra beans & other truck green

Go-devil or Mock if it wasn't theirs
was a "weathered gray-wood affair"
served him to write & title his tune
on Blue Note's *Whistle Stop* of '61

to Ira Gitler his tonal talk's romantic
but the tempo's far too fast & frantic
Philly Joe's skins so thunder & thud
it goes against setting a tender mood

maybe waited for her in shadows cast
by nighttime's one-eyed ogling moon
for "Sunset" with Hank Mobley's sax
sounds more evocative of rendezvous

with racism blatantly raising its head
in the street or wherever would trade
were kept in their place labeled shift-
less said rotgut & dice their only drift

to this Kenny perhaps a bit oblivious
for luckily able to sell all his buckets
of beans okra tomatoes & fresh juicy
plums to Watt Parker owned the city

& as head of the telephone exchange
gave KD a penny to fetch any person
received a call its 3-short-1-long ring
he answered even if not a Beethoven

in the 1890s on hauling corn by oxen
Watt letting horse & buggy pass him
but vowed one day he too would own
such a newfangled classy contraption

in later decades just two months after
the Market crash he'd open his dealer-
ship then have the gin & hospital built
better roads for selling his automobile

the banker-president of Fairfield State
chair of bond drive with world at war
attending '48 Convention as delegate
for Democrats & owned his 300-acre

plot with its weeds Ken had chopped
while his poppa handled for Mr. Watt
his four big young mules of top stock
drove too his new International truck

delivering workers to the highway site
20 miles distant brought hardly wealth
but relief as two-lane neared the white
rented four-room house sat up on stilts

living once in one-room shotgun type
with along one side their rowboat tied
for spring when Trinity River to flood
cover feral animals & cattle with mud

panthers or bobcats killed the old cow
desperadoes in making their getaways
ditched the stolen cars far out of town
in the land's lovely unending embrace

these the fragments he'd later jot down
rounding-ups led to his rhythmic drives
from calves cut out to notes like knives
not to carve but impart a sharper sound

delicious as Freestone County peaches
as stirring as Flash! Federal agents stop
interstate spree of cold-blooded thieves
satisfied in a way till he'd discover bop

with Bird & Cannonball ye-odle la-dee-
ing a cotton picker's very same melody
heard it on his dragging in his last sack
to weigh it & be paid a pittance of jack

their chases between a trumpet or tenor
non-violent exchanges with a rapid-fire
snare the alto bullets made none expire
while K's tones slay boomed or tender

yet before they could to leave the farm
move to Austin take music by the horn
learn to go unthrown by buckaroo lines
bulldog etudes & scales in record times

Westering

in '50 left Atlantic lit out for Pacific
debouching overland as Walter said
like Huck or a Forty-Niner but head-
ing out a century late to strike it rich

not picking rows as Okie or migrant
panning nuggets prior to Napa wine
but for a wife & two daughters sign-
ing on at a Republic's aviation plant

an ammunition dump over in Vallejo
in Oakland at the U.S. medical depot
later would part-time for a Jack Frost
sugar refinery any job to pay the cost

of clothes & rent not unhappy giving
up the horn as he needed to get away
split the scene & try the scenic living
escape an after-hours laboring by day

if not Polonius believed Mingus' line
on either coast one should be oneself
many K said wouldn't restock a shelf
hollered Freedom! Avant-Garde! fine

by him not to whine stuck to his guns
never to envy or covet fellow Texians
stars at Hermosa Beach with Kenton's
unit or Chet Baker at the Trade Winds

with Bird & Texas bass Harry Babasin
for KD didn't miss spotlight or crowds
felt lucky moving away from addiction
fool's gold lifts then drops from clouds

on leaving Bird in '47 Davis gave birth
to cool a Rugolo coin for Gerry's "Jeru"
& "Rocker" Miles' "Deception" Lewis'
"Rouge" the Gil Evans theory at work

as he & trumpet star aligned & altered
the energy levels boosted fused bop el-
ements for creating a 9-piece ensemble
orchestrated so light no soloist faltered

influence followed as Mulligan himself
went West his desert boots as "Walking
Shoes" & there's Shorty Rogers talking
Nonet too who next to his Giants an elf

his long trumpet lines like K's although
if not so daring nor intriguing yet swing
barely breathing so intent on his "Popo"
& so hell-bent on his "Apropos" to fling

caution to the winds to whirl as a dervish
with Jimmy Giuffre arriving from Dallas
huffing his tenor ever steady no nervous-
irvis rather his folksy "easy way" relaxes

yet drives home its simple loaded phrase
in '57 improvising *Suspensions*' notation
of tom-tom figure but first in '51 parleys
his '47 Herman hit into another iteration

of "Brothers" theme now "Four Mothers"
with Jolly Rogers in swashbuckling form
Jim a patch-eyed pirate takes no prisoners
he prodded on plank by Art's hooked arm

The Hero's Fall I Fell For

but just in fun as Hawes-Pepper pour it on
ignore a cross-boned yelling madcap crew
as K loads shells gunpowder a medication
pushes a dolly while meantime his embou-

chure slack out of practice lacking contact
with mouthpiece would touch it but's four
to feed has to eschew it & to face the fact
family's first yet an urge to more & more

while Ornette a fellow native low in L.A.
for an unheated garage cleans her kitchen
& baby-sits kids walks miles just to sit in
if he does asked "who taught you to play"

told to "learn the changes out-of-tune fool"
knows it isn't true & his keening the same
in '59 he & Ken together at Lenox School
teachers of the art before Coleman's fame

whose solo on his "Sphinx" a master class
of roaming the plains & trusting one's ear
its western pitches & slurs so hard to hear
for any afraid to venture into his fenceless

range's unknown sound foreign & strange
Kenny's own "D.C. Special" nothing new
his student group performing yet not up to
his then outmoded bop K chose to arrange

taking no chorus himself his a selflessness
allowed beginners their moment in the sun
as did some others Giuffre Roach & Lewis
a FreeFactory CD documents the occasion

K known too to share equally the solo time
on albums he'd make on his trips back east
in the years before his basking in that lime-
light rubbing innovators' elbows & at least

if traded no four-bars with harmolodic king
& unaware of him when the two struggling
to survive on golden shores assured a place
in pantheon bearing Ornette's name & face

neither a part of Frisco's jazz-poetry scene
Ferlinghetti doing "Junkman's Obbligato"
with local quintet his City Lights printing
Howl Parra's *Antipoems* Larry lifting "no

bird sang" from sonnet 73 Eliot also Stein
& Whitman & changed "Isle of Innisfree"
into Manisfree as from epitaph McMurtry
took *Horseman, Pass By* Yeats's final line

in '61 K to cut *Inta Somethin'* Pacific Jazz
taping him at the San Francisco Workshop
with altoist Jackie McLean student of bop-
pers from Bird to Mingus the angry Chazz

but if K in '51 not as Giuffre a Lighthouse
All-Star or in summer of '56 joining MJQ
for record at Berkshires Music Inn venue
in '52 Ken with Monk pre-Charlie Rouse

on "Skippy" & "Carolina Moon" coming
on strong a sort of hard-bop line removed
from Giuffre's "Fun" & a Lewis "Fugue"
or Milt's classical-drive 'harp a-humming

The Hero's Fall I Fell For

on all four Monk tunes recorded May 30th
K to do himself proud soloing on "Hornin'
In" & the lovely "Let's Cool One" & with
his ensemble work as bright as the mornin'

light as he joins with Lou Donaldson alto
& Lucky Thompson tenor on Thelonious'
rarely played his "intricate & treacherous"
"Skippy" & on southern waltz lunar glow

in Ken's later bag as *Down Beat* reviewer
to depict "odd but elegant" Monkish attire
of green sharkskin suit black shoes leather
skull cap & high priest's solo catching fire

in '60 K pictured on stage a Newport rebel
with Ornette & his white plastic sax beside
the bass of Mingus whose own Debut label
to issue K's first album in '53 with his side-

men Percy Heath bass Jimmy tenor Clarke
on drums Walter Bishop piano as K blows
& goes he & Jim in the flow on "Osmosis"
to bassist "Darn That Dream" never a lark

Percy ever serious & on "Ruby, My Dear"
K slows it down & then on "Be My Love"
speeds up with his patented staccato touch
Latin-like on "I Love You" his "An Oscar

for Oscar" the K original started things off
all proving him a hat-trick magician of bal-
lad or alla-breve rabbit stunts adroit at soft
loud fast slow high low or a swing chorale

in '52 as well with Percy's bass in a Sextet
Lou Donaldson led his 1st LP as he in hunt
with others to assume Bird's throne a front
line of Lou alto Gee trombone K's trumpet

Matthew a Texan too & on his 'bone quick
on the draw as Ken could be each's release
smooth as gunslinger cool-handed squeeze
on "Caracas" Gee the faster if have to pick

in '58 at George Wein's Rhode Island Fest
Giuffre filmed with own then featured Trio
Hall guitar Brookmeyer 'bone a subtle brio
"The Train and the River" the leader's best

at that rival Rebel concert Ken only caught
by recorders as his piano backed up Abbey
Lincoln singing her "Bizness" some said K
absconded with its funds perish the thought

generous to a fault charge should rather be
so think of K's daughters Keturah & Leslie
wife Rubina their later girls LeJuine Evette
& Lamesha this last perhaps Ken's favorite

for when was three he'd title a tune for her
he himself describes in notes to *Page One*
his first album with Joe Henderson's tenor
the two on their '63 session a father & son

his girls to visit by train Uncles & Aunties
to arrive as city-bred & prim young ladies
August Texas heat so primitive they cried
from stickers & as headless chickens died

to an NYC-born wife did K's "Stage West"
mean a thing if not ever in his dusty boots
never kicked around in his Post Oak roots
could she find in Giuffre's "Pony Express"

an appeal K'd feel for Jim's loping rhythm
or the least in his "California Here I Come"
perhaps could take JG's "The Quiet Time"
if it made *Quiet Kenny* to pop in her mind

though never named a song for her another
strong & tender mate juggling roles mother
housekeeper wage earner a keeper of home
fires burning a safe house a warm welcome

other women making do sewing patchwork
quilts of artful design bright African colors
sold to casual buyers or museums' curators
without any alimony deadbeat fathers shirk

an irresponsibility in no way meant to refer
to Ken's case nor a Monk's as "Crepuscule
with Nellie" written & titled for his skillful
half handled his tours trusted in her answer

if her opinion asked & as falcon Thelonious
turned & perned in gyres she would buy bus
plane or train ticket cook for his men bacon
& eggs Diz's too his tune for her "Lorraine"

K "Fragment" stops before Rubina's career
as a nurse back in NYC with its night shifts
the changing of sheets the rolling-overs lifts
bedpans emptied shots given in a hip or rear

the girls grown used to a metropolitan speed
crowded sidewalks high rises higher fashion
faster speech & a livelier scene greater need
to keep up with & have a piece of the action

difficult to feel attraction for his hostile land
dried creek beds grass burned coiling snakes
a whirring locust drove them mad said takes
natives to put up with racists wouldn't stand

never the twain shall meet can still hold true
despite the golden spike hammered together
east & west his marriage band never a fetter
if not his musical muse she'd seen it through

put up with his late-night hours tours abroad
home with reek of nightclub smoke thought
up & gave him the "Fairy Tale" title for ex-
tension of his "Epitaph" five of her own sex

& while Kenny ever tied by his nuptial knot
faithful to a coast-to-coast wedding of blues
& gospel with its have hard-bop cool-to-hot
orient-occident horn-will-travel Good News

Arriving

out of the chrysalis of bop & hard bop
K tries his wings in a '59 lower-keyed
Riverside flight with *Blue Spring* drop-
ping the temperature reducing the heat

to a balmy April day as he & Adderley
slow it down with less of Cannonball's
grandstanding sax & in his scoring KD
offers lusher lines his solo rises & falls

in "Spring Is Here" not above the staff
more often into earthier tones as tubers
root in a compost heap & as purple saf-
fron flowers from mold the cucumbers

watermelon sweet as bee pollen basket
keeps the cycle alive with KD's Septet
doing the same but minus pyrotechnics
just tendril-quick runs in his "Poetic"'s

tender strain as David Amram's French
horn warms the chords & Cecil's lyrical
baritone booms lighter with Cannonball
rushing before then letting go a drench-

ing rain of reedy notes a feeding of ears
with his kernels of gold nourish beyond
the metal itself a richer growth no pond
whose view to bream crop duster blears

by a chemical spray on one-time stream
had flowed pristine as his alto after K'd
come first with both testing the extreme
limits of a wind instrument each played

& though they've gone still blowing yet
through electric outlet amplifier speaker
set-up of mid-range with bass & tweeter
each's breeze a greening fruit-giving jet

Cedar Walton's piano at times Brubeck-
ian for like their leader a versatile Texan
Adderley at his best on "Spring Cannon"
K named for him on chases neck & neck

was it at this session he heard the altoist
yodel *la-d-odle la-d-odle* as he said he'd
heard the Bird before but first farm folks
after the sacks of bolls pulled & weighed

or off the range a cowboy at end of day
back at the corral uncinching his saddle
yet unlike sax K's horn not able to play
the *ye-o-dle de* yodel of cotton & cattle

on his "Passion Spring" he & C hand-in-
glove with Ken soloing down low again
yet more exploratory a Taylor influence
could be & a Cannonball deeply intense

on "It Might As Well Be Spring" K feel-
ing Rodgers' gay-melancholy lover tune
now truly sets his indelible staccato seal
on a fever season's never come too soon

in '58 having donned his teaching gown
on August 29 '59 his class goes to town
in Berkshires' Lenox School music barn
woods & hills once home to Hawthorne

& Melville too when he wrote his epical
prose if K didn't know Herman's Whale
or of humpbacked "inveterate composer
of song" the cetacean sounds of exposer

of danger above or a call below for love
in his way taught those to students from
Pete Farmer to trumpeter Don Cherry of
his/Ornette's *The Shape of Jazz to Come*

Ken saying of the Lenox mentor system
when he'd come to NYC had there been
such one-to-one instruction to show him
the ropes would have begged to be let in

as to the October 26 live Randy Weston
Five Spot session the less said the better
to a blue Monday add its dreary weather
its charts by a hospitalized Melba Liston

no time to run through a "High Fly" first
as Hawk & Roy Haynes' flights delayed
great tenor just warming up yet had paid
his dues could do that piece unrehearsed

together with K's horn a gorgeous sound
the two produce but in soloing over stop-
time piano chords Ken can be heard pop-
ping clams when he too had been around

for before & after KD's hooking up with
Bean another Coleman Hawkins moniker
out of a long '23 to then legendary career
the trumpeter a mainstay of saxophonists

of whatever persuasions from Swing-age
florid romantic to the Bird's cerebral bop
or the raucous soulful roar 'Trane so pop-
ularized with copycats taking up his gage

can count some three-dozen reed men K
had recorded with & wonder what other
trumpeteer joined so many from Mobley
Moody Rollins Monterose Heath brother

Jim to Land McLean Dolphy Henderson
leaving out an Ernie Henry lesser known
but K paired with any gave each his best
assisted all to shine on east coast or west

Oliver Nelson had never met when studio
called Ken to come in for the October 30th
quintet date with tenor from St. Louie Mo
had "been through the big band mill" with

units like the Nat Towles & Louie Bellson
always sitting in an alto chair till switched
to his larger axe though this lower weapon
heard to cut lyrically as that higher pitched

taking the edge off the bigger's harder bite
& making it into Jack Maher's softer quite
gentler carver his "salty dog" as on Ollie's
opener his own original "Jams and Jellies"

where KD plays his "pin wheels of sound"
needing the bread but ready to lend a hand
dependable in any supporting roles as here
he sustains "Passion Flower" "atmosphere

of [Billy Strayhorn] impressionism" while
tenor mixes slow & fast with "reverential"
in this ballad's "real" Ellingtonian "voice"
& with K muted the due respectful choice

then on "Don't Stand Up" K's open bright
happy tone perfectly matching Ollie's own
a rendering of his original theme o so right
& his break few tenors have ever outshone

O's "Ostinato" a fuller showcase for a KD
solo filled with an authoritative coming on
yet is equaled & even yes outdone by Ollie
pours it on with his quoting & snappy tone

as for "What's New" could say some more
but have gone into its loveliness heretofore
so add on "Booze Blues Baby" all at home
on this funky closing tune O's as if shalom

with November 13th *Quiet Kenny*'s arrival
as on this album with just his horn accom-
panied by piano bass & drums Ken's trum-
pet now to measure up in no sense of rival-

ry with any had proven their worth before
but brings to bear on a song a predecessor
had left his stamp upon a KD new-minted
responsive mood not a reading reinvented

the case with "My Ideal" a tune the Hawk
had cut in '43 & K had heard with "Body
& Soul" from '39 the tenor's peerless talk
via fifths tonic bridge a smidge of melody

but on that later piece Ken the one's more
moving with muted tones more than stack
up with a Bean's lush rhapsodic runs lack-
ing in K's restraint his passion never over-

done but with one deep-felt poignant note
his a voluminous speech as too a selective
Flanagan piano tone or a full chord of five
fingers can touch & leave a catch in throat

on his own "Blue Friday" K low & bluesy
an open horn altered as if muted or maybe
with a hand in bell his varied sound a case-
book blues prescriptive of phase or phrase

lovely the only word for Kenny on "Alone
Together" a tune for Maher closer to home
since K recalled his doing it first with Bird
here drops so low hits a rock-bottom nerve

with "I Had the Craziest Dream" Ken join-
ing the ranks of voices exceptional even in
a music as unique as American jazz whose
tongue speaks instant sense in pop or blues

bending his notes for their delicious blend-
ing of happy & hurt now making his mark
yet not as Harry James in '42 had depend-
ed more on soaring high as morning's lark

K rather digging deeper into emotive veins
exploring the subterranean subtlety of tone
in a melodic mother lode of the tune's own
harmonic mine layered with a lover's pains

& even if must doubt those overseas troops
would've sent in '43 their constant requests
from Canal or carrier or bombardier groups
for K's rendition of that song Helen Forrest

sang with HJ's band as soldier or sailor ded-
icated the Hit Parade lyrics to a pretty nurse
or the sweetheart hoped still waiting to wed
her snapshot publicity would never disperse

as it did that Betty Grable iconic pin-up shot
of her in her bathing suit leering back so hot
with her Lloyd's insured million-dollar legs
Harry married that year of nostalgia & pegs

while Ken's therapeutic lines would as well
have rehabilitated limbs or a wounded heart
if his light staccato soothing at a lower level
it lingers longer to lessen loss & being apart

& if not Warren-Gordon's tune K's Willard
Robison "Old Folks" version they'd ask for
again after he & Roach had played it before
in the plaintive slow swing impossibly hard

for those never achieving his effortless ease
a crackling concise unflashy & ever sincere
cantando telling of a corn-cob tale to please
& relieve to presto hope rallentandoing fear

if in his *Beggar's Opera* Gay seizes the day
sings "Beauty's a flower despised in decay"
his lyric itself as KD's album has yet to fade
as true songs survive on or off of Hit Parade

Satch's '55 "Mack the Knife" on that A side
of his single first to reach high as number 20
sold a million plus & not until "Hello Dolly"
did he hit top ten prior to the inevitable slide

Ken's of course cannot confuse with Louie's
whose vocal did the trick more than his horn
with its unmistakable its irrepressible breeze
ever blows its freshness & balm so unforlorn

letting forget for a moment a Brechtian shark
lying in wait with its pearly out-of-sight teeth
while K in modulating could dive underneath
to uncover light rays piercing a heartless dark

for as with Satch & Sonny Kenny too finding
even in such unlikely singing the silver lining
with Rollins in '56 turning a Weill's "Moritat"
from a deadly deed into his own colossal blat

on that jaunty violent song as on the Debussy
K beaten to the punch by S's whimsical tenor
& would be again in '57 on a Johnny Mercer
classic meant for Ken who outside the movie

of '36 when Bing had sung its satirical lyrics
knew *Rhythm of the Range* from real stirrups
no stunt-man routine of swingin' on a mount
& in a cloud of dust dashes right out of town

& unlike Teagarden's "I'm an Old Cowhand"
of that same year with lipped trombone turns
& melodious cords punching the witty words
K's is a sophisticated give-&-take self-call-&-

The Hero's Fall I Fell For

response lyrical asking-answering dialogue
with bent flutter-tongued half-valved notes
conversing both with an Andy Adams' *Log*
& Westminster chimes to Parliament votes

taking serious the Big Ben ring where Jack
in his vocal played up JM's amusing rimes
ranging up-to-date in Ford V-8 not no hack
no doggies roped got along to beef betimes

never back home whereas Newk on his sax
trail drives with cutting honks rawhide lash
a swing man skirts the herd to have it think
it's unrestrained fully free to graze or drink

on January 10th of '60 K takes over the lead
rides the point in heading the steers to cross
on solid rock not into muddy creek at a loss
of weaker stock & to turn cattle's stampede

into milling ends the run then bedding them
down on Mercer's English tune a KD brand
seared on top converted to a hard-bop hymn
an anthem to remuda quirt & the Rio Grand'

& afterward had he recorded no other cover
just as those Goodnight Loving & Chisholm
hoofprints're bound to be followed by lover
of longhorn lore this track on *Arrival* album

to stand ever a landmark of KD's musician-
ship since it alone if no other will surely en-
dure for showing clear as wagon-wheel ruts
his inspired breath-control his blood & guts

yet album offers too K's own "Stage West"
chased at breakneck speed as if by outlaws'
gang or redskin raid & "Song of Delilah"'s
a quieter muted K with "When Sunny Gets

Blue" to showcase Charlie Davis's baritone
leader's generosity become a second nature
though wish would've done it himself alone
except for rhythm as he did with the Mercer

& does with "Lazy Afternoon" as Flanagan
opens & closes with a hazy piano just quiet
enough to hear grass growing & daisies riot
as K mutes an unembellished melody again

& "Stella by Starlight" too on his *quiet* side
& then on Manny Albam's funky "Six Bits"
K & Charlie totally together everything fits
another winner from a gambler true & tried

the same two horns hooking up in February
on 11th & 12th to record *Jazz Contemporary*
six tunes in stereo for Time "For those who
dare" plus unreleased "Sign Off" in "exclu-

sive sound extra" the label declares pianist
now Steve Kuhn & on the first three out of
six issued tunes Jimmy Garrison as bassist
but on "Horn Salute" "Tonica" "This Love

of Mine" it's again Butch Warren & drum-
mer Buddy Enlow as too the month before
Kuhn's piano K had heard as an instructor
at the Lenox August '59 for Steve an alum

who then with Ron Brown comped behind
Ornette & Cherry on "The Sphinx" & "Inn
Tune" of Margo Guryan & who heard Ken
telling his students to be inquisitive to find

& learn formation of every chord & then to
run its scale & break it up into what makes
sense to get a rhythmic feel like land sakes
alive so top to bottom all you'll play is you

true of K who'd practice what he preached
as on his tune "A Waltz" on which he mad-
ly swings from a ¾ into 4 as alkali leached
from ash for b'iled soap as the granger had

Ken's "breathtaking swoop" Mark Reilly's
phrase "ringing" with "clarity & rich emo-
tion" while Kuhn surprises with his tempo
& feeling abruptly changed so fully please

if Charlie on bary squeaks a bit he was not
K's first but his second choice since Heath
couldn't make the gig but if Davis beneath
leader's excitement level he isn't God wot

with a gruffish yet tender tone on his won-
drous rendering of the Thelonious "Mood"
"Monk's" i.e. a most moving solo for con-
templation Kuhn's touchingly pensive too

the whole group tight & showing a proper
respect to one & all but K's show-stopper
chorus an authentic individuality "simmer-
ing" Mark's word with Monkish signature

in handkerchief corner "designedly dropt"
as Walt brought to a boil by that Emerson-
ian thought & to compose his *Leaves* from
reading "The Poet" when universe stopped

but on "In Your Own Sweet Way" Charlie
can't get started with Brubeck's tune cov-
ered in '56 by Miles & 'Trane though KD
had not heard that earlier version with lov-

ing muted tones from Miles' harmon push-
ing Eros' button the tenor's sweeping licks
unlocking melodic line without romantic's
mush yet amorous in his caressive whoosh

K more playful but sticking close to theme
as Miles did for to K too melody the thing
Bru by keeping away from clichés staying
fresh & K said liked bary as other extreme

to his own high notes while Kuhn to prove
adventurous here & on KD's "Horn Salute"
with its "choppy jagged" military phraseol-
ogy Kenny knew yet better bop's "Crazeol-

ogy" a Benny Harris tune Bird had maybe
played for Pannonica in those hotel rooms
where K rehearsed & from there could see
Hudson & Jersey hills whiff the perfumes

used in her mixed-media paintings of milk
acrylic & Scotch sketching then while Ken
& the men went over his "Tonica" written
for her as jazz Baroness whose Jewish gilt

The Hero's Fall I Fell For

took Monk in & who phoned a physician
for Bird felt his flickering beat heard thun-
der clap as Doctor came too late musician
gone yet alive on walls sound never done

though neither K ensemble nor solo lines
seem to recall his former bebopping boss
whose choruses had gotten by heart signs
missing it meant to revisit her day of loss

that weekend when she was looking after
a ragged Bird watched TV when laughter
at a juggling act on Tommy Dorsey show
broke blood loose choked & laid him low

earlier in '55 at Birdland in Ross Russell's
report Bud Powell is stewed Bird as well's
deep in his cups as Ken Blakey & Mingus
try to save the All-Stars date till KD tucks

his horn underneath an arm off to the side
of the cursing legends had befriended him
but now unable to help either one of them
ill past his cure must just move on if cried

back then or here in this nearly 3-minute
gift to her only with Butch's wistful bass
just a throb not a sorrowing sob no hint it
miffed KD when Bird gave Red his place

which leaves his CD's final piece his *sui
generis* rendition of "This Love of Mine"
with its fetching distinguished just lovely
tone his charming staccato so utterly fine

& same be said for the Harold Land date
of July 5th & 8th when as a stocking mate
perfectly matched to Houston-born tenor
San Diego-raised K & he one fitting pair

"so close" on their "So in Love" as Cole
Porter's lyrics say while Clarence Jones
on bass pushes & pulses & Ken's whole
solo's full of euphonious priceless tones

as he hits every note right on the money
undergirded on piano by an Amos Trice
a Joe Peters on drums two who not only
lend ample swing but more than suffice

with the pianist's own waltz the second
tune a piece he entitled "Triple Trouble"
& on which the horns together a fecund
duo sways in tune rich grain not stubble

on David Raksin's "Slowly" the tenorist
bringing out the theme of poignant love
then speeding it up for a blowing above
& beyond his solid work maybe his best

then Kenny still more touching yet light
in spirit as Trice turns in a splendid solo
of Clarence's bass chorus a simple ditto
with horns closing so romantically right

though "On a Little Street in Singapore"
it lacks aroma of a "lotus-covered door"
held in embrace by pale perfumed hand
no temple bells in K no exotica in Land

but back to their habitat in "Okay Blues"
can hear them at home with K's pinched
tone emotes in honor of Orrin Keepnews
here not a player would ever be benched

so KD arrived & on December 9th at last
tenor Jimmy Heath pianist Kenny Drew
Garrison bass & Art Taylor drummer do
another set for Time a Kern whistle blast

of light-hearted *Show Boat* tunes with all
aboard steaming along to Jerry's musical
with Hammerstein lyrics based on Ferber
her '26 novel with sidemen K would aver

the best he had picked for any albums yet
all hanging loose but with a surging drive
& with a refreshing vibe brings love alive
in songs Jerome had to pen with no regret

can hear in any why K had wanted Heath
but most of all in "Bill" when the tenorist
nearly steals the show as he flips & twists
& soars till Ken returns to win the wreath

with shifting tacks as in trimming of sails
for running the bow into wind for sudden
directional change a self-conversing nails
high to low close-hauled notes his caden-

za a trophy-cup end to the tune & session
began with "Why Do I Love You" telling
piano comping percussion unpell-melling
& bass pulsing a steady tasty punctuation

as tenor "full-throated" a K "more supple"
to quote Nat Hentoff's insert notes groove
alone or together a complementary couple
married by & unto jazz may none reprove

on "Nobody Else But Me" KD's bending
of tones Jimmy'll answer with a blending
of matching bends each filled with a feel-
ing for love's root chords harmonies heal

on "Can't Help Lovin' That Man" a ca-
pacity for gentleness flows this an alter-
ing of Hentoff phrase with K's unfalter-
ing expressive force a lyric emotive ca-

ressive rush a Mississippi pouring forth
as Williams wrote on Hernando's corse
later Crane's "hosannahs silently below"
in nearing docks the paddlewheels slow

to "Make Believe" & a stevedore Drew
not stomping as Duke but with keys un-
loading a *Cotton Blossom* not forgotten
"dartingly humorous" ever fresh & new

as flawlessly K states still lovely theme
his nuanced shapes & shades surprising
so & as only its metal & reed can swing
Heath's tenor renews any lover's dream

then horns together on "Ol' Man River"
toting barge & lifting bale to lend relief
to past injustice yet more would deliver
for here & now their firmly-held belief

no self should wish being someone else
& by riding the deepest current of Kern
to render its real & ideal tones & return
to dock to reveal them within all selves

just as Razaf's "Christopher Columbus"
sighted by the sextant in a sailor's song
so KD would see he hadn't gone wrong
to take tune & lyrics as a truer compass

pointed to the invitation soon from afar
to voyage abroad with blue minor scale
bag packed to travel with a musical tale
chord in head & fingers his guiding star

Zodiacing

June 4 of '68 nine days after the Summit
Barry Harris' Sextet with KD on trumpet
records *Bull's Eye* the Motown leader-pi-
anist's "shooting match" that's musically

speaking & Gardner's apropos liner notes
also say K's first record with Barry & his
friend Charles McPherson two associates
in Detroit latter altoist then but now totes

a tenor in session Don Schlitten produced
opens with the Barry title tune at extreme
up-tempo yet never too fast for a spruced-
up K who has in sight that targeted theme

lets fly first with his "superb articulation"
his speed & flow would've knocked Bird
out on remembering him from back when
he & Ken drovered together heading herd

Charles even compared with other Chazz
when he'd played on occasion a tenor too
as McPherson here & deserves such a ku-
do for handling that horn as well as he has

on baritone Pepper Adams can rarely con-
vince with his sound or sense though adds
a depth to ensemble's tone & PA has won
in Mark's liners a pat on the back ee-gads

here Barry recalls Bud Powell's phrasing
& chords in a sizzling chorus but's better
timeless could say on "Clockwise" where
it's just a trio with Higgins all're praising

& Chambers soloing arco is laudable too
while on "Off Monk" Barry with his bou-
quet paid to that prophet himself imitates
the rhythmic & tonal ways he deliberates

only a Pepper squeak to mar the homage
though made up for by K & tenor's com-
plementary play with trumpeter's engag-
ing lines relaxed but virile top to bottom

& McPherson reminding how the Mobe
could fit with Ken hand-in-glove & now
the tenorist swinging on a similar bough
another pea in a pod or a pinna to a lobe

on Barry's "Barengo" a "sinuous tango"
jazzed up by bary's anchor as KD leads
on this piece is after his heart with lingo
known from S.A. tour had planted seeds

clear from his later solo so relaxed once
more & yet all over his horn as he hunts
for & finds the Latin pulse he had heard
firsthand in New World Ken discovered

yet a land well known too to tenor man
who's conversant in its native speech as
even Pepper with his baritone more fas-
cinating with its slower "scorching" can

also be & a Harris piano with an almost
Kenton kind of "Peanut Vendor" riposte
& then a fine trio version of "Off Minor"
classic they render in Thelonious' honor

before they conclude with "O So Basal"
shows again why so many had invited K
to participate in recording sessions as all
knew could depend on him in every way

to lead or follow contribute a solo or sup-
port another's & never selfish not fanatic
of a single style neither manic nor erratic
with talent to spare but no way puffed up

his chorus a super display of every tech-
nique in his bag of tidbits his gift for sur-
prise ever delights no notes for the heck
of it & after the "pregnant pause" juicier

with tenor bary & piano all also offering
breaks "trenchant" or "spiky and mean"
a "hip" quote before Billy's drums bring
it home the last note Ken's long & clean

at the end of July on the 30th to be exact
KD to appear at NYC's Top of the Gate
with pianist Toshiko Akiyoshi a live act
of those + reed bass & drums still in '68

the first piece her own "Opus No. Zero"
nothing of Japan but of a "stop-and-go"
Blakey Messengers' "hard bop rhythm"
as on it Dryden's put a finger or thumb

with Ken himself as he carries the load
stating its theme with lift strong as ever
flexing his chorus as anytime he soloed
in chase takes on Lew Tabackin's tenor

& in playing "How Insensitive" straight
with Lew on flute after the piano embel-
lishes Jobim tune they like waves swell-
ing subsiding rise fall intensify or abate

for "The First Night" K more meditative
following the piano & flute in a classical
vein & before his-Lew-drum's explosive
notes break up a spell properly nocturnal

on "Phrygian Waterfall" Toshiko to solo
with left-hand ostinato keeps modal flow
but on her "gospel-drenched" "Let's Roll
in Sake" into Nat-Cannonball kinda soul

with a demanding part for Ken but never
anything to sweat for K for certain could
cut any given if no solo here will feature
him on their next tune as well she should

since K made "Morning of the Carnival"
almost his own not Bonfa's song a piece
he'd recorded at home & abroad & as al-
ways his flutter-tongue to lend new lease

on the listener's life & with his sixteenth
notes on Tosh's "My Elegy" his strength
& total control still intact his chorus fast
as any he played to play long as he'd last

Brownie lost to accident Lee to homicide
Booker to a kidney disease awaiting Ken
& on previous April 4th the assassination
of Dr. King same decade Kennedys died

Martin's eclipse under the astrology sign
of Aries the ram whose image on *Zodiac*
Donna Jordan drew first in order to align
her sleeve-art figures with monthly track

of the dozen constellations & second be-
cause 12/16/68 album begins with Cecil
Payne's in memoriam MLK on bass Wil-
bur Ware Al Heath drums Wynton Kelly

piano with Cecil on both baritone & alto
as KD pays tribute with his opening solo
to the Man who had his mountain dream
in Duke song lyrics none to tear its seam

not in Nashville not anywhere even if he
like Moses kept from that promised land
for thrown in Birmingham jail made free
at last all coloreds Jim Crow had banned

at times K's burred tone & slight vibrato
seem to sob for him his notes shudder on
coming down tremble a keen high to low
at others his lines lament & yet all blown

with his jubilating flow in celebration of
a life elected though aware it would lead
to a James Earl Ray out of belief in need
for non-violence justice & Christian love

on bary Payne carries on his own mourn-
ing for that peaceful protest marcher torn
away by the high-powered NRA's sacred
Second's right to bear Klan-armed hatred

Cecil's gruff low tones with Kelly's elec-
tric piano underscoring grief of Thoreau-
Gandhi disciples at fall of another heroic
follower yet comforted by where he'd go

far for sure from "Girl, you got a home"
& yet this second Cecil tune moving too
although in another way as he & Ken to-
gether besting K with any other baritone

their sound unmatched by either Adams-
K or Davis-K & in soloing Payne terrific
from beginning to end neither bim-bams
thank you mam nor quick flim-flam trick

& then a relaxed KD with superior swing
& more so again after a "pregnant pause"
as Kelly's chords contribute to the cause
for his unrushed blue notes keep it going

"Slide Hampton" a letdown where Ken's
concerned his brief break's not up to par
yet up to speed is Payne both his engines
firing first on bary then alto bar-after-bar

on "Follow Me" another Cecil up-tempo
his bary solo still more daring as now he
just lets go & how K takes in after him o
me o my with turns of phrases o so witty

& once Ware & Heath have traded fours
Al sets off alone to do his drummer thing
before the final piece the leader's "Flying
Fish" with pectoral fins for wings it soars

as does the whole quintet to a rumba beat
or some dance done in a Caribbean street
Cecil's bary solo lifted out of tropics' sea
& into flight by Wynton Wilbur & Tootie

while Kelly's piano chorus so plenty fine
& on ending the session K brings his feel
for the Afro-Latin rhythm with Al cosign-
ing the notes with subtly crashing cymbal

& then in spring of '69 Ken with thirteen-
year-old Donna's dad on Clifford's "new
phase" Dolphy series recording of "872"
recalls the tumultuous year's tragic scene

with another Tet attack & Black Panther
militant stand shooting of Huey Cleaver
in exile Hilliard too Seale Hoover F.B.I.
& near the end Hampton & Clark to die

but Ken just part of ensemble sound not
taking an in yo' face nor any angry solo
never one to complain wonder still what
he thought of radicals racist pigs & Mao

did he side in his mind more with a King
or with Carmichael's Black empowering
or reject imperiling his teeth as Satchmo
said he'd do no good if he couldn't blow

on his tenor Jordan now up to date on all
the enraged & raw-toned raucous school
ousts bop & fist-pumps death to the cool
but hear in his notes less hate than usual

& on Cliff's "Quagoudougou" the lower
tones on his horn his trill a sudden honk
& picked-off high-up pitch deliver more
of a point than any urge to bonk or conk

then K to work out his own "new phase"
yet after two kinds of bop no other craze
came natural to him though still to show
he could do it too & was willing to grow

his solo even so doesn't swing not up to
his older routine & Julian Priester trombone break nothing great while Wynton
with his groovy rock fits into old or new

two drummers Ed & Roy rambunctious
while the tenor's best here *In the World*
whose trend then Ken resided in for just
this once before eviction notice unfurled

with his final performance in August '70
his chops Yanow writes were failing him
on playing at Roosevelt College in memory of a Bird's 50th birthday anniversary

& never again would K record his sound
one never made on earth by any trumpet
even if better players to come had found
his horn or its brand none would make it

& even though he pauses more the spark
still there & on "Summertime" will hark
back to the old fire of those earlier years
with legends Yard 'Trane & all his peers

but first "Just Friends" with his scintillat-
ing runs & that burnished tone can never
mistake for another's can never overrate
its warmth or his ever getting it together

& then Ken introduces in his tenor voice
to be taped no more for the listener alive
the Gershwin as Ray Nance's violin jive
opens its bluesiness for which all rejoice

if KD's stamina's beginning to fade still
to hear him every trumpeteer must envy
the sustained power of an unbowed will
in honoring a mentor with such melody

remembering through every trill & tone
a note shaken up high held long or short
all the Bird solos he had gotten by heart
before arriving in NYC a near unknown

his mark made when his star would rise
if not in a CP sky jazz-gazers so idolize
& if not to inspire scrawls of "KD lives"
yet his a musical gift still gives & gives

Expiring

all the breaths once taken in & then let
out for words sung notes from trumpet
those tongued staccato or emitted long
for a sharp flat accidental natural song

the airflow divided up in bars of duple
triple quadruple time the tones to vary
in length & mood observing as a pupil
signatures for meter & to read the key

a life's continuum early middle & late
though still four years from fifty when
had to take work as a music-store ven-
dor & postal clerk with no record date

his cabaret card had lost & on dialysis
union dues unpaid membership expir-
ing meant no blood transfusion all this
while the girls grew up then NYU hir-

ing him as part-timer brought in some
& liked teaching but its pay minimum
had been to Austin for their Longhorn
Jazz Festival April 28-30 '67 perform-

ing with the Sam Houston State Band
had written for June *Down Beat* issue
his report on that event its who's who
from Monk Diz & Blakey to outstand-

ing fellow Texans Arnett Cobb Clean-
head Vinson Jimmy Ford Buddy Tate
Cedric Haywood & Charles Patterson
Teddy Wilson native hometown great

Ernie & Emilio Cáceres Larry Coryell
the Bayou City-raised Illinois Jacquet
plus drum legend Jo & the modern El-
vin unkin Joneses together for one set

of Jo wrote had played "with the ease
and grace that kings are made of" Art
"*fuerte y con mucho fuego*" & on part
of the young "White Power" 21-piece

"supporting cast" said for it & K boss
arrangements that audience screamed
his "what else?" shows never at a loss
for drollery as language too esteemed

even hoped to write or to play his way
to Diz's tremendous level & for '70 K
to produce indeed his so fine too-brief
modest memoir fragment's self-belief

the next year or the one after to phone
Austin's University to say might relo-
cate he'd enjoy playing in its jazz pro-
gram & helping band students to hone

their skills had plans for setting up his
treatments here D. Goodwin directing
the ensemble then & remembered this
who had arranged prior to K's passing

his "Epitaph" & performed that chart
at Chicago's national college jazz fes-
tival in '72 K December 5th breathless
from renal failure had stopped a heart

The Hero's Fall I Fell For

a brain filled with unseen notes heard
within his inner ears then out of tubes
a gold or a silver bell with valve lubes
had speeded along Messengers' word

a prophetic phrase blues or bossa beat
a chase or a smoky-toned running line
to blend with any instrument compete
with none but under the brothers' sign

Cecil Payne recalling at K's Brooklyn
family-man home he taught him a roll
& toodle on baritone looked sick skin
color *very* dry last seen at jazz mobile

studio where all there but Kenny grip-
ing about a musician's economic state
he *quiet* just holding his horn no hype
with him had accepted his chosen fate

had taken him from Post Oak to NYC
then 'Frisco Paree Scandinavia Brazil
to the lyrics learned & by them to feel
to the recorded sounds he will ever be

Acknowledgments

Black Flag, a One-Shot Poetry Bomb (1970) for "Leaders"

december (1971) for "Three Hayseed Musicians"

New Letters (1977) for excerpts from "Five Versions of the 'Twelfth-Street Rag'" (sections on Fats Waller and His Rhythm and on the Count Basie Orchestra with Lester Young)

New Texas (1995) for "Denton"

Nimrod (1971) for "Ornette in Rome"

Riata for "Letter to Dave Hickey" *(*1964); "Improvisations on the Notes of Akiko Yamaguchi" (1965)

Red River Review (2013) for "Jazz by the Boulevard"

Roundup: An Anthology of Texas Poets, From 1973 to 1998 (1999) for "María's Radio"

Seems (1974) for excerpts from "Music History" ("The Goodly Company in Chile" and "Pancakes & Prayers")

Stoney Lonesome #2 (1971) for "The Hero's Fall I Fell For"

The Dirty Goat #20 (2009) for "On Visiting NYC"

Wisconsin Review (1972) for "Martyrs"

The poems originally in magazines or anthologies, except for the two published in *Riata*, were reprinted in one or more of the following collections: *Brands* (Road Runner Press, 1972); *Taking Stock* (Prickly Pear Press, 1973); *Lines & Mounds* (Thorp Springs

Press, 1976); *Footprints, 1961-1978* (Thorp Springs Press, 1978); *María's Poems* (Prickly Pear Press, 1987); *Memories of Texas Towns & Cities* (Host Publications, 2000); *Backtracking* (Host Publications, 2004); *The Pilgrimage: Selected Poems, 1962-2012* (Lamar University Press, 2013); and *The Cowtown Circle* (Alamo Bay Press, 2014; 2016).

"On Visiting NYC," stanzas from "The Cowtown Circle," the Truman excerpt from "Presidential Doggerel," the New Orleans Jazz Band section of "Community Music Fest," "Boat House Grill," and "Serenading the Neighbors" are all from *The Cowtown Circle* (2014 or 2016). "Two Sonnets" is from *Footprints, 1961-1978*. The excerpt from "Jazz God & Freshman English" (on Harold T. Meehan) is from *Taking Stock*. Stanzas from "San Gabriel" are excerpted from *Austin* (Prickly Pear Press, 1985; reprinted in *Memories of Texas Towns & Cities)*, and stanzas from "Nixon" are excerpted from *Memories of Texas Towns & Cities*. "Professor Douglass Parker Keeps Charlie Live at the Harry Ransom Center" is from *María's Poems*. "Three Musicians Perform Their Freedom" and two excerpts from "Teachers at South Park High" (on Harold Meehan and James Manning) are from *Backtracking*. "Vikings in Reverse," "O-Yo-De-Lay-Hee-Hoing," "Westering," "Arriving," "Zodiacing," and "Expiring" are from *KD: a Jazz Biography* (Wings Press, 2012).

About the Author

Born in Fort Worth, Texas, in 1939, **Dave Oliphant** taught and/or edited a scholarly journal at The University of Texas at Austin from 1976 to 2006. In 2015, Wings Press published Oliphant's *Generations of Texas Poets*, a collection of his essays and reviews written over a period of 40 years, from 1973 to 2013. His most recent collections of poetry are *The Cowtown Circle* (a revised and expanded edition) and *María's Book*, both published in 2016 by Alamo Bay Press. In *Texas Books in Review*, Caitlin McCrory has written that "*The Cowtown Circle* takes readers on a journey across the physical, linguistic, and metaphysical landscapes of the imagination. Dave Oliphant's poems in his latest collection look for truth by meditating on the art of others. Oliphant moves from Stephen Crane to POWs at Camp Hearne to the [Modernism of artists in] the original cowtown, Fort Worth…Throughout this collection of eclectic work, Oliphant's lines have a musicality to them, reminiscent of Langston Hughes and Fats Domino.…What makes Oliphant's work so successful is his uncanny ability to get at what Tim O'Brien calls story-truth—the truth we know in our hearts." Also in *Texas Books in Review*, Zach Groesbeck has observed that "*María's Book*, a project that took forty-one years to finish, commemorates the golden wedding anniversary [of his wife's and his marriage in 1967]….The considerable time span of the collection's composition (coupled with the construction of the book) sets it apart from anything else in contemporary verse… Readers will notice Oliphant's disinterest in a sequential organization as the poems are arranged alphabetically…, rendering the book encyclopedic… [and conveying María] through her embodiment across a wider catalog of her belongings and her actions."

www.ingramcontent.com/pod-product-compliance
Lightning Source LLC
Chambersburg PA
CBHW021437080526
44588CB00009B/574